Good Value

STEPHEN GREEN

Good Value

Reflections on Money, Morality and an Uncertain World

ALLEN LANE
an imprint of
PENGUIN BOOKS

ALLEN LANE

Published by the Penguin Group
Penguin Books Ltd, 80 Strand, London WC2R 0RL, England
Penguin Group (USA) Inc., 375 Hudson Street, New York, New York 10014, USA
Penguin Group (Canada), 90 Eglinton Avenue East, Suite 700, Toronto, Ontario, Canada M4P 2Y3
(a division of Pearson Canada Inc.)
Penguin Ireland, 25 St Stephen's Green, Dublin 2, Ireland (a division of Penguin Books Ltd)
Penguin Group (Australia), 250 Camberwell Road, Camberwell, Victoria 3124, Australia
(a division of Pearson Australia Group Pty Ltd)
Penguin Books India Pvt Ltd, 11 Community Centre, Panchsheel Park, New Delhi – 110 017, India
Penguin Group (NZ), 67 Apollo Drive, Rosedale, North Shore 0632, New Zealand
(a division of Pearson New Zealand Ltd)
Penguin Books (South Africa) (Pty) Ltd, 24 Sturdee Avenue,
Rosebank, Johannesburg 2196, South Africa

Penguin Books Ltd, Registered Offices: 80 Strand, London WC2R 0RL, England

www.penguin.com

First published 2009
1

Set in 10.5/14 pt Linotype Sabon
Typeset by Rowland Phototypesetting Ltd, Bury St Edmunds, Suffolk
Printed in England by Clays Ltd, St Ives plc

ISBN: 978-1-846-14236-9

www.greenpenguin.co.uk

Penguin Books is committed to a sustainable future
for our business, our readers and our planet.
The book in your hands is made from paper
certified by the Forest Stewardship Council.

*To Heather, James, William, Andrew and
my other grandchild as yet unborn.*

Contents

With Special Thanks to ... ix
Exploration xi

1. In My Beginning is My End 1
2. The World's Mine Oyster 20
3. The Global Bazaar 48
4. The Home Stretch to a New Jerusalem? 81
5. From Tulips to Sub-Prime to ... 107
6. Why Should I Do Anything for Posterity? 134
7. Faust and the Rich Young Man 161
8. In My End is My Beginning 183

Acknowledgements 206

With Special Thanks to ...

Richard Addis, who has worked so closely with me on the writing of this book. He is the great-grandson of Charles Addis, who was in many ways the face of the Hong Kong and Shanghai Banking Corporation in China in the late nineteenth century.

My connection with Charles Addis is that I have worked for twenty-seven years for HSBC, partly in Hong Kong and partly in London.

Charles Addis had a highly successful banking career, and, after his return to London in 1905, became increasingly involved as an adviser to government in international financial negotiations, both before and after the First World War. He was also keenly interested in literature and culture, and was a deeply religious man. His convictions underpinned everything he did. He believed strongly that international financial stability was essential to world peace. And he never believed that commerce could thrive without integrity.

He once wrote that 'the ultimate basis for all economic conceptions is ethical.' He was right.

I could not have written this book without Richard's invaluable support.

In addition, my heartfelt thanks go to Brian Griffiths, who read the draft not once but twice, at different stages of its evolution, and provided a wealth of ideas and strong encouragement; to Lesley Perry and David Walsh, who brought fresh eyes to the text and suggested crucial refinements; to Helen Conford, the commissioning editor, who brought all her experience to bear in support of an amateur at book writing; to Sara Dare, who helped greatly with the logistics of getting the book finished; and of course to Jay, who readily and patiently puts up with me in the midst of her own busy life.

Exploration

This book is a journey of unfinished exploration by someone who has spent much of a working lifetime with money, commerce and economic development. It begins on a weekend at the Villa d'Este on Lake Como in the beautiful Italian spring of April 2008, against the background of an unfolding global financial crisis. It became a time of reflection – about a system that suddenly seemed to be built on sand instead of rock, about the whole direction of human economic and social development, about the ambiguity of the human experience of it all.

The questions all this poses were never more important than they are now. We are at one of those moments in history when it seems as if the tectonic plates are shifting. We are living through years in which a crisis has overtaken our increasingly globalized world, such as most of us have not seen in our lifetimes. The questions strike at the root of what we have taken for granted for at least a quarter of a century. There has been a massive breakdown of trust: trust in the financial system, trust in bankers, trust in business, trust in business leaders, trust in politicians, trust in the media, trust in the whole process of globalization – all have been severely damaged, in rich countries and in poor countries alike.

And if trust has been broken in this way, where do we go from here? Questions arise about the system. How to fix it? Should we/can we turn the clock back? What are the alternatives? Questions also arise for us as individuals. What part did we play in what went wrong? What do we do in the future? And, beneath it all, what have we learned about ourselves as human beings? About what constitutes good business and a good life? About what our values are? About what the common good is?

To face these questions, we have to begin with recognition. There are lessons to be learned, both collectively (globally) and individually. Renewed progress depends on our being willing to learn; hope depends on a determination to gain in wisdom through it all; and wisdom will be found to depend on an honest search for the good. But this is not a book about economics or policy. It is not a recipe for the reform of the global economic or financial system. It is about the other kinds of issue which arise from a global crisis of historic proportions: questions about who we are, about how we have changed, about our beginnings and ends. It is an exploration which is topical now, but is in fact always necessary, in all times and places. We are, however, more conscious of the questions when times are stressed – as they have been of late. We need to take time to face them, face up to them.

Such an exploration inevitably has to start with taking stock of where we have come from. The first part of this book therefore reflects on the astonishing impact of globalization on human history and consciousness. We cannot understand our present dilemmas except in this context. The second part of the book seeks to look forward and inward (and I believe we cannot do the one without the other). Since it has to look inward, the exploration is therefore inevitably both personal and provisional. Each person's journey is incomplete, and it is his or her own, of course – and yet we have so much in common too. The questions resonate widely: What is happening to our world? What's the point of the work I spend so much of my creative energy on? What do I want to leave behind? Is there anything more to it all than 'life, liberty and the pursuit of happiness'?

I

In My Beginning is My End

We shall not cease from exploration
And the end of all our exploring
Will be to arrive where we started
And know the place for the first time.
T. S. Eliot – *'Little Gidding'* (1942)

Lake Como. Spring 2008. April. Eliot's cruellest month. Twilight falling. From the shore, the lights of Brunate in the distance are just beginning to flicker into life. Shadows lengthen in the gardens of the Villa d'Este.

Everywhere the soothing influence of the pleasure principle is clearly in evidence. Despite all the beauties that nature provides in Lombardy without any human intervention, there is very little here that has escaped the improving hands of painters, architects, gardeners and sculptors.

With names that sound like expensive puddings, luxurious retreats line the shores – Villa Carlotta, Villa del Balbianello, Villa Melzi, Villa Serbelloni. The lake has entranced the cream of European aristocratic and cultural circles for two millennia, from Pliny to George IV to Stendhal and Liszt. The Villa d'Este at Cernobbio, commissioned in the sixteenth century by Cardinal Tolomeo Galli, is now a luxury hotel. Under vaulted ceilings, past statues of sleeping nymphs and over gravelled paths, the guests come and go. If the story of humankind is how far we have come from the freezing cave and the daily chase, then here at least it is easy to forget that either ever existed.

Why am I here? Another seminar on commerce and finance: another of those Davos-like gatherings that bring together the usual suspects – politicians, financiers and economists – to discuss the state of the world. Champagne and discretion. The rain-makers of global capitalism can wander among the azaleas, camellias, oleanders, rhododendrons, hydrangeas, roses and jasmine bushes, and confide their fears and hopes to each other. It is a time of retreat, and a time to share. A place to relax, to take stock, perhaps to plan, perhaps to deal.

This year, more so than anyone can remember, the mood is bleak. The rumble of approaching economic thunder is the basso continuo of all discussions. Over ten years of growth and untrammelled consumer expansion may be coming to an end.

Nobody should be surprised. All over the world the economic news has been foreboding.

A new double-barrelled word has entered the conversation, spreading fear like a sort of plague. This word is 'sub-prime'. Two years ago, most members of the public had never heard of it. At the Villa d'Este it is on everyone's lips. Already several hundred billion dollars have been written off by financial institutions as a result of mortgage-payment defaults and huge write-downs of mortgage-backed asset values. The figure is to get much larger. US banks have just reported the worst quarterly performance since 1990. Banks in the US, the UK and Germany have had to be rescued from collapse and lost their independence. And much more is to come.

The scale of the unfolding crisis is alarming. The International Monetary Fund has delivered one of its gloomiest forecasts ever. It says bluntly that the troubles that erupted into the open in August 2007 now look like developing into the largest financial shock to the system for decades. It predicts that the liquidity squeeze will lead on to a full-blown credit crunch in the advanced economies. It predicts recession in the US later in the year, and only slow recovery thereafter. It says that weakening growth in advanced economies will have knock-on effects on the large emerging economies, particularly in Asia and Latin America. It concludes that the heady growth rates that the world has come to take for granted are – at least for the time being – a thing of the past.

Worrying, too, is the parlous state of consumer confidence. There is wide agreement that the housing sector is in serious decline in several advanced economies. After many years of rapid price increases, with all the confident investment and spending which result, real investment in housing is now falling in countries as diverse as the United States, Britain, Australia, Spain and Ireland. The US Commerce Department has just released figures showing that the number of new houses remaining unsold in the US is now at its highest level in a quarter of a century.

At the same time there are increasing fears of inflation, for the price of oil is soaring. Consumption is forecast to increase relentlessly by 1.2 million barrels a day this year, to a new record of 87.2 million barrels a day. Prices are at record levels – flirting with $120 a barrel – and yet supply is not rising. In the US, experts are predicting a rise to over $4 a gallon at the gasoline pump by the end of the summer and, according to one, $7 a gallon in the next four years. More worrying still is the apparent paralysis of supply in the non-OPEC countries, such as Russia, Norway and Mexico. Strikes by oil workers in Nigeria have shut down around 1.7 per cent of the world's production. How will all this end?

And there is an even worse spectre abroad: food prices. The United Nations Food Agency is warning that, across the world, escalating food prices threaten to force 100 million people to go hungry. Analysts are predicting that the days of relatively cheap food are over. Rice prices have already nearly tripled in a year. Wheat and vegetable oil are due to continue their steady rise. In poor countries there are food riots. More are predicted. Even in rich countries the effects are noticeable. In Britain, *The Times* devotes an entire front page to the report that food price inflation has pushed up the average weekly UK shopping bill by 15 per cent in a year – not life-threatening, but quite enough to sour the mood of any electorate.

In this mountainous corner of European civilization, this showcase of some of humanity's finest artefacts, we are feeling the first tremors of an economic earthquake. No one is going so far as to say that the walls of the citadel will come tumbling down. However, no one is going to guarantee its perpetual stability with quite as much confidence as they might have done just a year earlier.

And it is not only the actors of the financial world who are affected. Shocks to the global financial system will eventually affect us all, from suburban families in America to small businesses in China, to Greek shipowners and to Russian oligarchs.

Somewhere deep down, the question gnaws away: If, with all the technology and sophistication at our disposal, the basic structure of the world economy is built upon sand, not rock, then what is the justification for all our labours? For all of us who work directly or tangentially in the financial system, how can everything we relied on be so swiftly under threat?

Milan. The world capital of pizzazz. The Piazza del Duomo. The same spring 2008. The same April. Midday. All the life of the city seems to gather here, along with many of Lombardy's pigeons. Palatial nineteenth-century buildings flank two sides of the spacious square. Giuseppe Mengoni's soaring 30-metre high shopping arcade, the Galleria Vittorio Emanuele, a cathedral of commerce which has become home to Gucci, Prada, Louis Vuitton and other minor divinities popular in Italy, emerges on to the square through a triumphal archway. In the midst of the piazza is a statue on horseback of Vittorio himself, Italy's boisterous first king. Underground, though, are the foundations of the fourth-century Basilica di Santa Tecla, where St Augustine had been baptized sixteen hundred years before. And then, drawing all eyes and dominating the space as powerfully as if it were a vision of paradise, the breathtaking architectural masterpiece of Milan's duomo, an extraordinary tracery of stone and glass rising majestically through the spring sunshine.

Good journalist that he was, Mark Twain noted his first impression: 'What a wonder it is! So grand, so solemn, so vast! And yet so delicate, so airy, so graceful! A very world of solid weight, and yet it seems ... a delusion of frostwork that might vanish with a breath.'

I have left the Villa d'Este a few hours early to pay homage to one of the largest and most beautiful churches in the world. Immediately the contrast strikes deep. I have come from a place of luxury and calm, albeit threatened and undermined by the distant drumbeat of impending economic instability. And I have arrived in the heart of a modern Italian city, nearly 4 million people living amid a tangle of medieval streets, nineteenth-century confidence and twentieth-century functionalism, vibrant, volatile and vivid, the very embodiment of energetic instability, yet where the main symbol is a building of such ethereal transcendence that it makes the present economic and financial disturbances seem like nothing more significant than duck down floating on the tide of history.

All the more remarkable, then, to ponder the conditions out of which this monument arose. Few would dispute that the latter decades of the fourteenth century were some of the darkest, most unstable years in Europe's history. When the then archbishop of Milan, Antonio da Saluzzo, began work on the duomo in 1386, Europe was going through one of its most dangerous phases. The Little Ice Age and, even more dramatically, the bubonic plague had laid waste to the intellectual and agricultural progress of thirteenth-century Europe, spreading starvation, disease and despair throughout the continent. In the countryside, marauding and desperate gangs searched frantically for food and shelter.

During the middle years of the fourteenth century the Black Death spread rapidly through France, Spain and Italy, and then crossed the Channel into England. In some areas mortality was as high as 90 per cent. The first wave of plague swept through Europe between 1347 and 1350, and in the next fifty years there were six further waves. By 1400 most estimates agree that the population of Europe had probably been cut by at least a third. Life has rarely fitted Hobbes's famous description so closely: 'solitary, poor, nasty, brutish, and short'.

Alongside this boiled other troubles. The Hundred Years War plunged much of France into turmoil until 1453; the only cohesive social force in the continent, the Roman Catholic Church, was seething with corruption; there were rival popes in Rome and

Avignon; anti-Semitism was rife; and there were regular hysterical outbursts of violent witch-hunting in order to try to root out the supposed causes of all this distress. To imagine a building project such as Milan Cathedral being launched against a backcloth of such turbulence is extraordinary to say the least.

Nor was it just the beginnings of the project that were battered by the storms of history. Officially the cathedral was not completed until 1965. In the intervening 579 years since the first stone was laid, embellishment and renovation continued through upheavals and cataclysms as powerful as any in the world. The very conditions that made Milan prosper – its strategic significance in one of Europe's richest and most fertile regions, its geographical position at the head of Italy near the gateway through the Alps, and its rapidly increasing artistic treasure trove – made it the object of many an aggressor's attentions. And yet, as invaders battled on the Lombardy plains and new rulers passed through the royal and religious palaces, the cathedral endured.

Not that this was a straightforward case of the spiritual world triumphant amid the storms of human history. This building was always the result of mixed motives, with the human yearning for God and for Mammon (and the human lust for power) in the tight and tangled embrace that we have always known. Yes, the cathedral was built to the glory of God and for the edification of the faithful. But it was also built to establish the political dominance of Milan and its ruling families over the surrounding dynasties.

In Milan's endless struggle with the neighbouring cities of Bergamo, Novara, Cremona, Como and Lodi, the cathedral became an increasingly important symbol. Milan's regional hegemony was in the end undefeated, but then broader European struggles enveloped the city. In the early sixteenth century northern Italy became a battleground between the Spanish and French. In 1535 Lombardy became a Spanish colony, and for 170 years Milan became the neglected capital of a distant provincial outpost.

In the early eighteenth century the Austrian Habsburg Empire took control of the area and revolutionized Milan's economic, cultural and administrative structures. Napoleon invaded triumphantly in May 1796, but even before his death Lombardy was returned to Austrian hands by the Congress of Vienna of 1814–15. The Milanese agitated constantly against their Austrian rulers, but it wasn't until 1859 that they managed to oust their occupiers and become part of the Kingdom of Piedmont, which two years later evolved into the Kingdom of Italy. The Fascist Party was founded in Milan in 1919, and it was from there three years later than Mussolini started his March on Rome. It was in Milan that Mussolini, his mistress and fifteen leading Fascists were hung upside down from the Esso station in the Piazzale Loreto on 29 April 1945. During the later stages of the war, British and US bombers had targeted the city heavily: but amid the destruction, the cathedral and its priceless contents were virtually unharmed. Today, it stands there still as the symbol of . . . what?

From across the square it looks like a forest in stone. Pinnacles sprout from every column. More than 3,500 statues crowd the exterior walls. The roof is crowned with a mass of spires and gargoyles. At the main west entrance, the doors swarm with marble, low-relief sculptures of birds, insects, fruits and animals so vivid as to seem alive.

Once inside, a coolness and a calm descend. Deep shadows are everywhere, and the darkness is deepest at the centre, under the spire, where a huge crucifix hangs in the gloom. Cutting through the darkness are shafts of light, prismatic and even ethereal. The eye travels through the shade and around the columns, across the intricate stonework, and along the sweeping high-beamed roof, but it is always drawn ineluctably to the light, to the great stained-glass windows at the east end, often repaired but still bearing much of the same design that was put there in the fourteenth century, and much of the same glass.

And as the glittering Milanese spring sun streams through the glass into the perpetual twilight of the interior, we are drawn to the image of the sun that sits in the centre of the pattern – a deeply ambiguous image representing at once the eternal ideal of the light of God's truth and at the same time the very temporal might of the Visconti family, who paid for the window and whose family emblem was the sun.

No cathedral is more overtly an emphatic statement of political power than Milan's. But there is also no mistaking the mysterious directions in which it points – inward to an inner darkness, and outward to the brightest of light.

Oxford, 1968. The middle year of three spent studying Politics, Philosophy and Economics – the year when you didn't have to work for exams, either your prelims or your finals. A year when it really did feel as though Oswald Spengler's decline of the West had begun. It was the year of the murder of Robert Kennedy (he who had quoted George Bernard Shaw's 'Some look at things that are and ask why? I dream of things that never were and ask why not?') It was the year of Martin Luther King's murder too ('I have a dream . . .'). It was the year of the Prague Spring – and then of the Russian invasion in August. Throughout, there was Vietnam: weekend after weekend, buses took students down to London to demonstrate in front of the US embassy in Grosvenor Square. And, hanging over everything, there was the Cold War with its threat of Mutual Assured Destruction. It was a year when dreams and hopes seemed to be snuffed out one after another. It really did seem if some sort of apocalypse might be at hand.

Mentally travelling back forty years, from Lake Como and Milan to reading PPE among the spires of Oxford, how dramatically *simple* those days seem. This isn't just the added historical perspective, or even that being young made everything seem possible then. They really were the days when big issues were deeply contrasted, the days of clear polarities, when all seemed black or white. Everything was either exciting or outrageous. There was nothing to be indifferent about.

Today, the fervour seems to have all but disappeared. We have seen 1989 since then. Today the old left/right divide is widely believed to have faded away and to be on the verge of replacement by a grey ideology-free centre ground. In the spring of 2007, the monthly magazine *Prospect* asked a number of commentators to predict what idea would define the twenty-first century as the notion of left and right had defined the twentieth. No one disputed the implied premise.

The writer A. S. Byatt forecast a consensus populism, with policies driven by mass polling and focus groups. The film critic Mark Cousins similarly saw all political decisions being made by daily and weekly referendums on the internet. Will Hutton, the author and journalist, saw the big divide as being between liberals and fundamentalists. For all the respondents, the political and intellectual future was grey – or perhaps multicoloured – but in any case no longer black and white. Overall, the mood was pessimistic. Almost nobody expected the world to get better. So many seemed, in the words of T. S. Eliot's Magi, 'no longer at ease . . . in the old dispensation'.

On the wider global stage the contrasts are sharper still. In the 1960s the Cold War was at its height. The US House of Representatives official congressional record for 10 January 1963 contains a record entitled 'Current Communist Goals', placed there as a warning to the American people. They look like a silly caricature now, but presumably people genuinely feared them at the time. They include the aim of overthrowing all colonial governments throughout the world, discrediting the family as a social institution, encouraging easy divorce and promiscuity, infiltrating big business and the unions, dismantling the FBI, and belittling all forms of American culture and the teaching of American history. It was the decade of the first Nuclear Test Ban Treaty, and the beginning of years of counting warheads and watching missile deployments. In those days you grew up knowing that sufficient nuclear missiles were pointing in your direction to ensure a swift demise if world war broke out again. Schoolchildren knew the opening lines of Peter Porter's famous poetical two-minute warning:

> Your Attention Please
>
> The Polar DEW* has just warned that
> A nuclear rocket strike of
> At least one thousand megatons
> Has been launched by the enemy
> Directly at our major cities . . .
>
> *Distant Early Warning.

Today the simple polarities of the old East/West divide, which gave way to the upheavals of 1989, the break-up of the Soviet Empire, and the (temporary) era of a single, dominant, US, superpower, are fast being replaced by a far more complex geopolitical reality.

Established patterns and structures are transforming themselves, and we do not know what will be the outcome. However, broad outlines may be emerging. More than half of global GDP growth is now produced by the developing world. The centres of power and influence henceforth will not just be the US, the EU and Japan, but will include China, India, Russia, Brazil and the Middle East. Trade, culture and geopolitical relations will become exponentially more intricate as money and ideas flow in an ever-increasing variety of directions between countries.

In business, too, how much simpler the equation used to be. It was in the 1960s that Milton Friedman, an economist at the University of Chicago, published *A Monetary History of the United States, 1867–1960*. The book caused consternation by accusing the American Federal Reserve of being chiefly responsible for the Great Depression. What, at the time, passed with somewhat less comment were Friedman's uncompromising views on business. He was the apostle of the pure profit motive: 'There is one and only one social responsibility of business – to use its resources and engage in activities designed to increase its profits so long as it stays within the rules of the game, which is to say, engages in open and free competition without deception or fraud' (*Capitalism and Freedom* (1962)).

Today we live in a world where business has complex loyalties and responsibilities, and is subject to continuous pressure not only from shareholders but from government, media, special-interest groups, regulators and litigators. Friedman's view would now be considered dangerously simplistic. These days business must consider a far more subtle range of interests and needs. It must consider value from the perspective not just of investors, but of customers, employees, suppliers, communities and – increasingly – the environment too. There may have been a time when business leaders were masters of all they surveyed, when their power was untrammelled, when 'the business of America was business,' as Calvin Coolidge put it. Today, however, they are actors on a much more crowded stage, in a much more complex drama.

The loss of easy certainties has a profound effect on people. The psychologist Viktor Frankl has written movingly in his book *Man's Search for Meaning* about his three years in Nazi concentration camps. He went on to develop a school of psychiatry based on the will to find meaning. His approach ascribed many of the anxieties of modern man to a twofold loss. First, and long ago, there was the surmounting of our primeval animal instincts, which had given total psychological security by removing all choice. Second, and much more recently, there was the rapid disappearance of the communal traditions which buttressed behaviour and taught us what to do in so many of the most important life situations.

The past fifty years have seen a swift acceleration of this loss of certainty. Frankl saw this as inevitably leading to two major compensatory neuroses: the will to power (of which the lust for money is really just a manifestation) and the will to pleasure (in which sex becomes an obsession and libido becomes rampant). Neither of these neuroses – both of which have been obvious in contemporary life – is new of course. But behind them lies a pervasive malaise: the sense of drift experienced by so many in developed societies in which most people have moved beyond the daily struggle for subsistence. Perceived increases in the incidence of clinical depression since the Second World War, however hard to confirm, are arguably evidence of this underlying anxiety. The dawn of the twentieth century in the richer countries was characterized by a Chekhovian wistfulness about an illusory (and in any case doomed) golden age. But societies then knew what progress would mean, even if it made them uncomfortable: in *The Cherry Orchard*, the brash merchant Lopakhin is the essence of the new commercialism and urbanization. The sound of the axe being taken to the cherry trees is the sound of progress.

The second half of the twentieth century had a more ominous tone, set by Orwell, Kafka and Beckett – who has the character Vladimir in *Waiting for Godot,* his most famous play, express the bewilderment of twentieth-century human experience in this way:

'What are we doing here, *that* is the question. And we are blessed in this, that we happen to know the answer. Yes, in this immense confusion one thing alone is clear. We are waiting for Godot to come.' But Godot never comes.

What is the icon of anxiety for the twenty-first century? We will have to wait to see. But for many in the older developed world, and also in many countries released from the communist/totalitarian straitjacket in 1989, the dilemma is clear. These societies have seen the cherry orchard disappear. Progress has come. What has replaced it does not satisfy the will to find meaning, and they have lost any sense that Godot might come.

Kolkata, India. Dalhousie Square. It is a pitch-dark night sometime in 1988. The temperature is 33 °C, and the humidity is 85 per cent. Tim is returning to his parked car after an outing to an after-work drinks party. A former British public-school boy, he has done broadly what he was brought up to do. After completing his education, he went into the City. Now he is a branch manager of an international bank, posted to India as part of his career development. He has a large flat, a cook, a good salary and a smart car. It is the car that has attracted a small swarm of children tonight – some of the tens of thousands of street children who scrape a living in this seething capital of West Bengal.

As Tim approaches, they start to protest. Why did he leave his car in the dark? If anything happened to it and he complained to the police, did he not realize that the police would blame them? By leaving his car unattended like that, he had put them at risk of arrest or, at the least, of a beating.

Unlike most Westerners, indeed most adults, who live and work in the old capital of the British Raj, Tim stops. He squats on his haunches and speaks to the children. He offers to let them sleep on, under and inside his car in future, as long as they protect it from thieves. The children can scarcely believe their luck. As the unusual Englishman drives off, they ask themselves, Will he keep his promise?

He kept his promise. And more. Later, when one of the children fell very ill, Tim took the child to a doctor, a client of the bank's. The child needed a haven to recover, and Tim took him back to his flat. Gradually other children joined the first. It was not long before thirty street children were taking up every inch of his home. Realizing that its young branch manager was spending more time looking after street children than banking, his bank recalled him to its head office in Hong Kong. Every weekend he would fly back to Kolkata to attend to the children. It was not long before he resigned to found his charity Future Hope.

He has stuck to it through thick and thin, through successes and failures – seeing children grow up and succeed beyond anything they could have imagined, seeing some go to universities, seeing some run away, sometimes seeing children die – for twenty years. Today Future Hope cares for over two hundred children.* Tim is married with three children of his own. He and his wife, Erica, regard the street children as a sort of extended family, and life is often chaotic and unpredictable and disappointing. But infinitely rewarding.

St Otiep's Orphanage, Kayole, Kenya. May 2007. Not a place which features in the guidebook. A young Australian trainee accountant, James, stands pale and blinking in the dust of one of Nairobi's most notorious slums, the stronghold of the Mungiki, Kenya's mafia.

Rubbish burns in piles on the side of the road, wild dogs wander the streets; there is no sanitation to speak of, and little electricity. The orphanage has seven rooms, and houses twenty young children. There are three classrooms, two teachers, a handful of old textbooks using the wrong syllabus, a hole in the ground for a toilet, a bucket for a shower, a cupboard for a kitchen, and two bedrooms with one bed in each room. In the boys' room each night, four squeeze on to the single mattress and eight sleep on the concrete floor. The arrangement in the girls' room is the same, except that the caretaker also squeezes on to the bed.

James has taken a four-month break from his training to travel the world with a friend. The plan was to hike in the Himalayas and tour western Europe, after starting with some volunteer work in

*The full story and details of the charity can be found at www.futurehope.net.

Africa. A chance conversation over the internet led to a flight from Sydney to Nairobi and a bus to St Otiep's. Within days they decided not to take the rest of the trip. The European drinking money goes on extra beds, textbooks, cooking equipment and clothes for the children.

In September, James has to return to his training in Australia, but before leaving he meets with the matron and two teachers at the orphanage and lets them know that his support will not end: he will work something out over the next twelve months. Not long after returning home he receives an email from a local Kenyan friend: 'James, four days ago the director kicked the kids on to the streets of Kayole, changed the lock and walked away. The teachers couldn't even get their bags out. He's sold everything, even the textbooks . . . St Otiep's is finished.'

With a friend, via phone and email, James organizes a bus to get most of the orphans out of the city to a small village, called Mang'u, about an hour from Nairobi. They hire a small house for $60 per month and name it the Familia Moja Children's Centre. (*Familia moja* is Swahili for 'one family'.) In March the following year he arranges extended leave from the accountancy firm and returns with his girlfriend, Heidi, for two months. He is determined to find the eight missing children from St Otiep's that never made it on to the bus. They track down six of the eight, and bring them to the new orphanage. James works tirelessly to organize funding and support.* Today he can say that the twenty-four children in the orphanage have a full-time social worker, matron, assistant matron and orphanage manager to take care of them; they all get three meals a day, special tutoring after school, their own bed, clean drinking water, and shoes.

Pondering the stories of these remarkable-yet-ordinary people challenges me. It challenges us all, surely. If they are so clear about their priorities and their responsibilities to do something for the world, if they have the courage to give up comfort and safe structures

---

*He has established Kick Start Kids International as a charity in Australia in support of Familia Moja.

and take such risks, if they are prepared to take their own families and children with them or spend holiday times, or even lifetimes, among some of the most abused, neglected and exploited children on earth, why not others? Why not I?

Is it that we are all too risk-averse? Is it that we have no moral convictions about our duties in the world? Should we be in some way ashamed for staying with what we know and enjoying the relative luxury of our lives?

Maybe we are so satisfied and at ease with the immediate pleasures on offer that we have made the decision to still our conscience in return for a nice car and a detached house and exotic but risk-less holidays. Maybe we have made some kind of Faustian bargain. If we allow all these thoughts to gather momentum, we could be forgiven for feeling surrounded by challenges on all sides. Facing us is the challenge of the Villa d'Este: that even the richest, most sophisticated economic system the world has ever known is after all dangerously fragile. Behind us is the challenge of Milan Cathedral: that even in the midst of chaos and squalor, and driven by a cocktail of deeply mixed motives, humanity can raise extraordinary monuments to the mystery of being. To one side is the challenge of modernity: that all the old certainties and support systems have given way to a world of seemingly infinite confusion and complexity, leaving us feeling adrift. On the other side is the challenge of individual choice: that you can, if you're brave, give up security and go to help the poor and the forgotten with your own hands. And whispered in our ear, perhaps, is the sotto-voce question of whether our small lives and labours add up to anything of significance anyway.

Why *do* we do what we do? If I listen, the question is insistent. Yet there is no answer which satisfies. Not if an answer implies something simple and definitive, for such an answer is bound in the end to be unconvincing. And yet there is perhaps a response – and one which I believe can ultimately be deeply rewarding.

But before I reach it, there are some things which it is essential to accept. There can be no true response without assent to certain fundamental realities. They are perplexing realities, but nothing of what follows in this book can make sense without them. Call them three ambiguities. They are, I believe, deeply woven into the fabric of experience, and finding real peace depends on being able to accept and live with them.

The first ambiguity lies in the nature of imperfection. It is this: we are idealistic beings, driven to create ideas and objects and to do things of great purity and beauty. We are deeply drawn to these ideas and objects and actions. And yet, the very moment we make ourselves part of them, we seem to find that they are – or become – flawed. There seems to be an unerring tendency in everything we are part of to fall short of ideals and to be imperfect. Indeed, this imperfection can sometimes take on very sinister forms, as we shall see later. Hints of this are there in that interior darkness in the cathedral. Imperfection is deeply part of us, and we are a part of it. We cannot escape from this.

The second ambiguity lies in the nature of the end of human progress. The old Victorian sense of progress ever onward and upward has given way to a much more uncertain sense of where we are heading. What is the outcome likely to be? You can make the bull case or the bear case with about equal conviction. So there is an ambiguity about what the end of it all will be. Climate change brings this into a sharper focus, as did the nuclear arms race in middle of the last century (with the difference that climate change is a slow burning fuse, whereas the spectre of nuclear catastrophe had a unique immediacy about it). As life around us improves, and standards of health care and education and recreation all steadily progress, the thought must remain: The world could be less good for our grandchildren. Will we ever get to the point where the job is all done, where humanity has reached a stable, comfortable, peaceful, shared existence on a planet which is sustainable, where individuals are at peace with themselves and each other? Will we get to that, or will there be a different kind of destination: flood and fire, pandemics, conflict on a previously unknown scale?

The third ambiguity lies in the nature of hope. I believe this is the most significant of them all, and the central ambiguity of our existence. It is this: we know that evil is widespread in the world, and yet we believe that something better is possible – we go on hoping, often in the teeth of the evidence. For the most part, in the tortured words of the poet (and priest) Gerard Manley Hopkins, we do 'not choose not to be'.

Even in the darkest times in human history or in our own lives, there still seems to be the recurrent possibility of making the assertion (even though it may at the time be groundless) that hope will endure. We may not know at all what grounds we have for believing it. Why in the midst of awfulness would we believe it? And I am not talking about naive hope. The hope we may find in the midst of evil is not a material hope of a kind which holds that life will get better or that progress is inevitable: it is a hope that is as strange as the evil we know to be endemic in our experience. Can it meaningfully be the response to the question: Why bother?

Spring. East Coker, Somerset. A village of fewer than two thousand souls, and the setting for the second (and greatest?) of T. S. Eliot's *Four Quartets*. Eliot's ashes lie here, in St Michael's, the village church. It was from this village that his ancestors emigrated to Boston, Massachusetts, in 1660.

It is a picture-book English village. The church is twelfth century. The only significant dwelling, Coker Court, is a fifteenth-century manor now divided into several homes. The honey-coloured stone soaks up the sun during the day, and then at dusk it glows with released warmth. It feels like an England caught in amber – though it is in fact only just outside the expanding, bustling town of Yeovil.

Eliot's ashes are commemorated by a simple plaque in the church with the words of his self-selected epitaph, the opening and closing words of *East Coker*:

> In my beginning is my end.
> In my end is my beginning.

Those words 'beginning' and 'end' are what Eliot's great poem ponders. For Eliot, beginnings are not just physical or geographical origins – though they are that too, and very importantly. They are also where we start from by conviction and assertion. And ends are not just where the story finishes, but the purpose of the journey, the reason why we make it, and what we discover on the way.

So the mystery that Eliot ponders is how ends are always embedded in beginnings. As soon as a child is born we are guaranteed another death. The suggestion that he explores in the poem, however, is that it is not just physical ends that are inherent in physical beginnings. To lead a complete human life we must, in another sense too, accept that our end is in our beginning, that we will find our purpose in our roots, and that our beginning is in our end, that we will find our roots in our purpose. Often enough it seems that our lives are mere exercises in serendipity, with very little connecting thread running through them. A large part of our quest as humans is to explore what we can come to accept as our 'home' in the profoundest sense, for that is where we will discover our true spiritual purpose.

Compartmentalization – dividing life up into different realms, with different ends and subject to different rules – is a besetting sin of human beings. We all want to present many versions of ourselves – different faces for different others (and even to ourselves in different moods or at different times). 'There's no art to find the mind's construction in the face' – but we know even our own minds only imperfectly. From the sinister to the trivial, we are tempted to compartmentalize. From the camp commandant who could recite whole passages from Goethe's *Faust*, to the office politician and family man, to any of us who have ever put on a face, two-timed, time-served, pursued anything at all costs, sold our souls: we are all guilty in some degree of compartmentalization.

Compartmentalization is a refuge from ambiguity; it enables us to simplify the rules by which we live in our different realms of life, and so avoid – if we are not careful – the moral and spiritual questions. One of the most obvious and commonplace manifestations of the tendency to compartmentalize is seeing our work life as being a neutral realm in which questions of value (other than shareholder value) or of rightness (other than what is lawful) or of wisdom (other than what is practical) need not arise. But there are many other ways too in which we compartmentalize our lives. Work, family, friends, society – these are different (though often partially overlapping) realms of life, and it is all too easy, in a thousand ways, to play to different rules in each of them. These different realms of being also overlap with the inner realm of the self (though none of them completely): by what star does that inner self navigate? And would it even know when it is off course? Compartmentalization helps to shut such questions out.

But in the end, if we want to explore ourselves, we cannot limit the field where we search. And we must explore, if we are to discover – or rediscover – our beginnings and ends. It is clear what the goal is. A response to the question (singular and plural): Why do I do what I do? Why do we do what we do? And it is also clear what the prize is. As Eliot puts it in 'Little Gidding' (the last of his *Four Quartets*):

> We shall not cease from exploration.
> And the end of all our exploring
> Will be to arrive where we started
> And know the place for the first time.

2

The World's Mine Oyster

FALSTAFF: I will not lend thee a penny . . .
PISTOL: Why then, the world's mine oyster, which I with
    sword will open.   William Shakespeare,
                      The Merry Wives of Windsor (1602)

*To be fully ourselves it is . . . in the direction of convergence
with all the rest . . . that we must advance – towards the
'other'. The peak of ourselves, the acme of our originality,
is not our individuality but our person; and according to
the evolutionary structure of the world, we can only find
our person by uniting together. There is no mind without
synthesis.*   Pierre Teilhard de Chardin,
                    The Phenomenon of Man (1955)

*The new electronic interdependence recreates the world in the
image of a global village.*   Marshall McLuhan,
                    The Gutenberg Galaxy (1962)

We have become too used to globalization. In fact it has become
a cliché in the public mind, even while analysts and historians try
to explain it. Is it new, or is it old – perhaps as old as the human
species? Is it the conscious design of some self-appointed global
elite? Or a Frankenstein monster gone out of control? Is it cultural
cross-fertilization, or a global dumbing down? Does it lead to growing understanding and respect, or to growing tension and conflict?

Above all, is it progress or not, and should it – can it – be stopped or not?

The new millennium started out in a flush of confidence in an increasingly globalized world. In 2005 a book was published that immediately caught the mood of the new century. *The World is Flat: – A Brief History of the Globalized World in the Twenty-first Century* was written by the three-times winner of the Pulitzer Prize and columnist in the *New York Times* Thomas Friedman. From the start it was a runaway bestseller. Within two years it had sold over 2 million copies. An expert on international affairs and economics, Friedman used the book to extol the triumph of free-market capitalism over the state-controlled communist economic model. His basic thesis was that the contemporary explosion of advanced technologies and the consequent connecting of knowledge and resources all over the world meant that we are all potentially equal competitors with each other.

The book was a journalistic tour de force. At its heart was a ten-point list of 'flatteners' that had changed the world. They included great events such as the fall of the Berlin Wall on 9 November 1989, technological innovations such as the launch of the first web browser in 1995, and the burgeoning new trends of open-sourcing, out-sourcing, insourcing and supply-chaining that took place throughout the 1990s. 'Turbo-charged' by the emergence of a true web-enabled global playing field, massive new strides in international commercial collaboration and the sudden arrival in the marketplace of 3 billion new competitors from China, India, Russia, eastern Europe and Central Asia, these flatteners, Friedman argued, had brought the world to a 'tipping point' at which change had become exponential and irreversible.

On that foundation, Friedman built his argument. As he considered the differing abilities of various countries to adapt and prosper in the 'flat' world, he developed a view that a crucial factor in allowing the spread of ideas and best practices around the world was the ability of a culture to absorb foreign ideas and influences. The more absorbent a culture, he said, the greater its advantage in a flat world. His examples of highly absorbent cultures were India,

America, Japan and lately China. He also included some Muslim countries, such as Turkey, Indonesia and Malaysia, but by contrast he argued that some others, such as the majority of Arab societies, had found it difficult to benefit from the advantages of a flat world. Friedman's suggestion was that, as power was diffused and distinctiveness became harder to sustain, *Homo economicus* was becoming more and more alike everywhere.

And not just more alike. One of Friedman's most widely discussed ideas was that nations would also become more peaceful. He encapsulated this in his 'Dell Theory of Conflict Prevention'. The 'Dell' part of it was happenstance: he was using a Dell computer to write the book. Knowing that it was a machine of many parts that could not have existed at the price he paid for it without extensive outsourcing, it occurred to him to find out where it had come from. He obtained the entire supply chain from Dell's head office. As he gradually discovered where every single building block of the assemblage came from – the microprocessor from the Philippines, Costa Rica, Malaysia or China; the memory from Korea, Taiwan, Germany or Japan, and so forth – he pieced together an extra-ordinary picture. The pattern that emerged was a huge multinational logistical and communications web. Friedman was keen to update his previous 'Golden Arches Theory of Conflict Prevention', which had stipulated that when a country reaches the level of economic development where it has a middle class big enough to support a network of McDonald's, it becomes a McDonald's country, and people in McDonald's countries don't choose to fight wars any more. (They prefer to wait in line for burgers.) The Dell theory went further by saying that the advent of global supply chains was an even greater restraint on geopolitical aggression. It held that:

No two countries that are both part of a major global supply chain, like Dell's, will ever fight a war against each other as long as they are both part of the same global supply chain. Because people embedded in major global supply chains don't want to fight old-time wars anymore. They want to make just-in-time deliveries of goods and services – and enjoy the rising standards of living that come with that.

Friedman's image caught the mood of the age. The idea that multinational corporations could actually help bring world peace was too good to disbelieve.

However, late in the first decade of the twenty-first century, after the onset of major global economic upheaval, we already feel older and wiser, less inclined to see the earth as 'flat' or the opportunities as so limitless and widespread.

First, it is now clear that the competitive and wealth-creating opportunities that Friedman enthuses about are still relevant mainly to small, urban, educated elites. Richard Florida, Professor of Public Policy at George Mason University in Virginia, has shown in some detail how the international economic landscape is, by almost any measure, far from 'flat'. When looked at through the lens of economic production, there are relatively few cities that generate innovation, and these are separated by 'vast valleys' with almost no connection to the global economy and few immediate prospects of benefiting from it. Drawn in this fashion, the map of the world appears 'spiky' rather than flat. Florida argues that the leading city-regions in terms of creativity currently number fewer than ten: London, New York, Paris, Tokyo, Hong Kong, Singapore, Chicago, Los Angeles and San Francisco – clusters of economic creativity which are strongly connected to each other, but only feebly connected to the rest of the world. Even though other cities are probably poised to join this network (Shanghai, for example, is clearly on its way to becoming a world city), it remains responsible for only a small fraction of economic activity or human interaction more generally. Its sheer dominance of world creativity on almost any measure is unlikely to be reduced in the foreseeable future. The world is surely not 'flat'.

Second, Friedman overestimated the ability to be creative in isolation. There is now a lot of work on innovation that shows how interaction and the proximity of fellow 'creatives' are crucial to the rate of innovation. In particular, Nobel economist Robert Lucas has shown how difficult it is for ideas to flow as freely or to be honed as sharply when people are scattered in their homes and workplaces.

Third, there is now enough evidence from studies such as the World Values Survey covering the last two decades of the twentieth century to show that diversity is not in fact declining, as Friedman suggested, and nor are loyalties becoming more global. By contrast, what seems to be happening is that, during the initial industrialization of an economy, cultural values *do* start to become more homogeneous, driven by shared materialism and an emphasis on economic growth at almost any price. But as soon as countries become 'post-industrial' (defined as having the majority of the workforce employed in the service sector – which happened in the US in 1956) the priorities quickly refocus on quality of life, self expression and such issues as environmental protection. This often goes with an actual renaissance of cultural diversity and regional loyalty – sometimes even seeming to generate more awareness of diversity than ever existed before.

Fourth, the 'Dell theory' doesn't bear the weight that Friedman put on it. Many have pointed out that the historical evidence is against it. US companies invested hugely in Germany before the First World War. Likewise, between the wars, there was a rash of specialized banks and law firms that focused on opening the German market to US capital, and none of this prevented the Second World War. And we shouldn't forget the potential darker side of commercial interconnectedness. Terrorist networks may well use it for the purpose of destruction, not profit. In the world of the web, the transmission of terror and the expansion of criminality also become easier.

In fact, the antecedents of the notion that trade and investment can prevent conflict go back some way, and when looked at more thoroughly they provide serious cause for doubt. One long and detailed examination of the subject was by the economist Karl Polanyi. In 1944 Polanyi published *The Great Transformation*, the book for which he is chiefly remembered. In this he focused on the breakdown of the 'one hundred years of peace' – the century of harmony that began from the time of the Battle of Waterloo and which saw the Industrial Revolution gain momentum in Europe, the US and then Japan. The latter decades of the nineteenth century saw unprecedented growth in world trade and in overseas investment from Europe into Asia and the New World. It was widely believed that progress was unstoppable and that there were too many vested interests in globalization for war to be rational any longer. In fact, of course, the balance of power in Europe (and in Asia as Japan's economic and military might increased and its regional aspirations became more marked) was precarious, and the competition for empire was becoming more aggressive. But there was nevertheless a prevailing optimism about the power of progress and the international market to secure the peace.

Today it is hard to imagine just how secure that peace felt at the time. Had we been living in the first decade of the twentieth century we might have read an article in the 1913 edition of the *New York Times* without any disbelief or cynicism. The headline trumpets confidently, 'INVITE ALL NATIONS TO THE PEACE PARTY'. The story beneath talks about an international celebration to mark the centenary of the Treaty of Ghent, which had originally been signed on Christmas Eve 1814, to end the War of 1812 between the US and Great Britain. This celebration, said the organizers, would make clear that 'the time has come when international rivalries and differences, though numerous and severe, may be settled without the carnage and horrors of war.' All the great powers were to be present, and expensive solemnization plans were on the table. But by the summer of 1914, not surprisingly, the 'peace party' was forgotten.

The task Polanyi set himself was to explain the political and economic origins of the collapse of this peace and of the great transformation that he had lived through in the twentieth century. (He knew what he was talking about, for he had experienced the First World War as a serving officer in the Austro-Hungarian army.) As he saw it, four institutions were crucial to the economic and political peace that had characterized the nineteenth century: a balance of political power, the international gold standard, the liberal state, and a self-regulating market system. Of these, he believed the self-regulating market was 'the fount and matrix of the system', and the 'innovation which gave rise to a specific civilization'. However, one of his main conclusions was that the market does *not* in fact guarantee peace and stability alongside prosperity. Polanyi argued that self-regulated markets, in whatever context they may occur, give rise to a spontaneous counter-movement, even among those enjoying increased material prosperity; they contain the inevitable seeds of conflict and breakdown within them, because the market will always try, as he put it, to dominate social structures. As a result, there will sooner or later be dislocation and a massive counter-reaction.

This was profound and prescient, as we shall see later. Viewed from the perspective of the early twenty-first century, there is no reason to believe this analysis is outmoded. For we are now living through just such a period of massive dislocation, brought on precisely because – in Polanyi's terms – the market has tried to dominate social structures.

Lucid and provocative, Friedman initially seemed to many to have captured the essence of the economic possibilities of the twenty-first century. His book was published, in 2005, on the crest of a wave of optimism. It was a wave that even then was about to break. Perhaps influenced by some of the criticism that depicted him as a cheerleader for corporate capitalism, blind to the conflict and greed that can always be found in capitalism's closet, Friedman subsequently darkened his outlook. In September 2008 he followed up *The World is Flat* with another book, *Hot, Flat and Crowded: Why We Need a Green Revolution and How It Can Renew America*. In this he argued that the economic future was shifting from information technology to renewable environmental technology, that the 'Cold War Era' was morphing into the 'Energy-Climate Era', and that the world would shortly be dominated by the problems of growing demand for scarcer supplies, massive transfer of wealth to oil-producing countries, disruptive climate change, an increasing wealth gap, and an accelerating loss of biodiversity. He warned of an approaching turning point in around 2050 beyond which it would be impossible for humanity to reverse the harmful affects of climate change, and mournfully pondered America's loss of focus and national purpose.

As time has gone by, Friedman's thesis that the world is 'flat' has come to seem simplistic and superficial. However, there is another vision of globalization that is more subtle, more perceptive, and which perhaps begins to get us closer to some kind of answer to the question from the last chapter about beginnings and endings.

The Phenomenon of Man by palaeontologist, philosopher and Jesuit priest, Pierre Teilhard de Chardin was published posthumously in 1955, fifty years before *The World is Flat*. *The Phenomenon of Man* is not an easy book. During his lifetime, Teilhard's Roman Catholic authorities banned its publication because of what seemed to be its questionable and ambiguous ideas. It also infuriated rationalists, who regarded it as pseudo-scientific mumbo-jumbo. Teilhard himself admitted that many would finish the book unable to decide whether he had been 'leading them through facts, through metaphysics or through dreams'. And yet it stands the test of time as a strangely more prescient and compelling vision of globalization than Friedman's.

In *The Phenomenon of Man*, Teilhard fuses scientific under-standing and visionary imagery to lay out the steps of a theory of human evolution. As he was a palaeontologist, it is no surprise that he starts much further back than Friedman – his first chapters are about the evolution of matter. Key to all his thinking is the image of the world as a sphere, not just literally but metaphorically. He sees the evolutionary ascent of human beings as happening in two stages. In the first stage, humanity expands around the globe, gradually covering the sphere with its presence until it meets up with itself and begins to know itself more fully. By the twentieth century, with most of the habitable earth populated, the second stage begins. A kind of tapestry of ideas weaves itself around the earth, and a collective memory is developed. Human mental activity overlaps, interconnects, converges and begins to unify. A complex membrane of thought, fuelled by human consciousness, seems to envelop the globe. He describes the process as 'a gigantic psychobiological operation, a sort of mega-synthesis, the "super-arrangement" to which all the thinking elements of the earth find themselves today individually and collectively subject'. And he compares this 'super-arrangement' to 'some great body which is being born – with its limbs, its nervous system, its perceptive organs, its memory – the body in fact of that great living Thing which has to come to fulfil the ambitions aroused in the reflective being by the newly acquired consciousness'.

To distinguish it from the stage of evolution which produced the biosphere, Teilhard called this stage of evolution, this collective network of mind, the 'noosphere' (from the Greek *nous*, meaning 'mind'). Others since have seen in this image a prefiguring of the vast electronic web of the internet, encircling the earth and connecting humanity from its remotest corners, creating one living sheath of continuous communication and thought – 'A Globe, Clothing Itself With a Brain', as an excited headline in the June 1995 edition of *Wired* magazine put it. But this is to trivialize his vision of human evolution, which foresees a profound change in human consciousness and in our understanding of the nature of being.

Teilhard predicted that, as people became more self-aware, evolution would speed up. He envisioned a planet whose material evolution was slowing down at the same time as an exponential growth took place in the sharing and refinement of ideas that would eventually free humanity from the individualism intrinsic to physical-ity. A new type of conscious existence would come into being, which he called the 'Omega Point'. He is at pains to stress that at the heart of Omega is a 'secret complicity between the infinite and the infinitesimal' – a convergence of the individual and the universal. He believed that, to be truly itself, humanity must advance in the direction of convergence rather than 'drag the world backwards' by fighting for individuality and singularity. The peak of evolution was not individuality but *person*. And to be fully a person could only mean leaving conscious and assertive individuality behind: 'according to the evolutionary structure of the world we can only find our person by uniting together.'

In his hypothesis of humanity ascending from matter to spirit and from separateness to union, Teilhard is certainly mystical and optimistic; yet he is not naive. He does not ignore the dark side: 'As things are now going it will not be long before we run full tilt into one another. Something will explode if we persist in trying to squeeze into our old tumble-down huts the material and spiritual forces that are henceforward on the scale of the world.'

In the conclusion of *The Phenomenon of Man* he confronts two possibilities about the maturing of the humanized world. One possibility is that evil is reduced to a minimum and what he calls 'the final convergence' will take place in peace. But there is also another possibility, in which 'Obeying a law from which nothing in the past has ever been exempt, evil may go on growing alongside good, and it too may attain its paroxysm at the end in some specifically new form.'

Teilhard's thought-world is not easy to enter. His vision of human development can easily seem nebulous. But I believe he has glimpsed something which few others have sensed so perceptively. He has seen that globalization is about something far deeper than economics, commerce and politics. It is an evolution of the human spirit. And, on this view, the end of globalization remains radically open precisely because of the ambiguities that seem to be intrinsic to the human spirit as it evolves.

Can we, or should we, interpret Teilhard's sense that evil may go on growing alongside the good in terms of a 'clash of civilizations' as foreseen by another influential contemporary voice, the political scientist Samuel P. Huntington? In his *The Clash of Civilizations and the Remaking of World Order*, published in 1996, he wrote that 'the fundamental source of conflict in this new world will not be primarily ideological or primarily economic. The great divisions among humankind and the dominating source of conflict will be cultural ... The clash of civilizations will dominate global politics. The fault lines between civilizations will be the battle lines of the future.'

Huntington divided the world into predominantly cultural or religious groupings. There were, he said, eight civilizations that qualified as 'major': Western, Orthodox, Latin American, Hindu, Muslim, Sinic (China, Korea and Vietnam), Japanese, and the civilization of sub-Saharan Africa. Clashes, when they came, would arrive in two forms, he said: 'fault-line' conflicts and 'core-state' conflicts. Fault-line conflicts happen between adjacent states that belong to different civilizations. Core-state conflicts happen between the major states of different civilizations. Fault-line conflicts often foreshadow core-state conflicts.

The thesis clearly has some force. In a European context, for example, the fault line that runs through the Balkans is a very ancient one; the disintegration of Yugoslavia since 1991 certainly looked like a (three-way) clash of civilizations (Western, Orthodox and Muslim). And, more generally, some of the most terrible experiences of the last century were motivated at least in part by a desire by the aggressors to assert their civilization's superiority (Japan's invasion of China in 1937, Nazi Germany's invasion of Russia in 1941).

But it is hard to see in the clash of civilizations the dominant theme of human contention in history. More basic causes of political and military aggression – such as competition for land, water and energy – underlie most past conflicts; and indeed these threaten to become more important as causes of instability in the future. Huntington's categorization of people along broadly cultural and/or religious lines is surely far too one-dimensional.

In fact changing patterns of self-definition are one of the most striking features of the present day. How many people today define themselves by membership of just one group or category? People's identities are not only complex, but becoming more so. To take just one person's experience: even in purely geographical terms, my own identity is multilayered. As a child, I grew up in a British seaside town and its surroundings (Brighton and the South Downs). The sea and the Sussex countryside will always be part of me; they are part of my beginnings, and at the end I would like my ashes to be scattered on the Sussex Downs. But there is another layer of my identity too: I am European. My home is a continent which is not just a geographical entity (of which the British Isles are a part, even if many on those islands prefer to think otherwise) but a cultural tradition and a shared history. And then – in between the very local and the continental – I am something else that, in a manner symptomatic of a particular British problem, I find a little hard to define. (Am I English or British?) I also know that my identity needs to be open to the wider world if it is not to become ingrown and sterile: as Kipling put it, for people, and not just for the English, 'What should they know of England who only England know?'

The Indian Nobel Prize-winning economist Amartya Sen generalizes this point in his 2006 book *Identity and Violence: The Illusion of Destiny*. Sen was born in West Bengal, and became the first Asian academic to be master of an Oxbridge college before moving to Harvard. He personifies many overlapping identities, and many loyalties. His book is surely much nearer the truth about the complexity of the human spirit than is *The Clash of Civilizations*. Sen points out that people can be grouped in multiple ways, each of which may involve deep ties and powerful meaning for the individual: nationality, location, class, occupation, social status, language, politics, among others. He argues that religious or cultural categories, despite their frequent prominence in public discourse, do not negate other categories of belonging, nor can they be seen as the only relevant classification system. In fact the reductionist view that a human being can be adequately labelled by religion or culture not only encourages 'clashing', but prevents genuine attempts at dialogue. A failure to see the many overlapping identities of humanity limits discussion to the areas of disagreement. Sen argues that Western attempts to promote ties with the Muslim world can too often seem like a pair of friends who have many things in common but only want to talk about the one area where they deeply disagree. He calls for greater recognition of the full range of links that have woven people together across divides of religion and nationality over the centuries, including the arts, literature, science, mathematics, sport and trade:

People see themselves – and have reason to see themselves – in many different ways. For example, a Bangladeshi Muslim is not only a Muslim but also a Bengali and a Bangladeshi, typically quite proud of the Bengali language, literature, and music, not to mention the other identities he or she may have connected with class, gender, occupation, politics, aesthetic taste, and so on. Bangladesh's separation from Pakistan was not based on religion at all, since a Muslim identity was shared by the bulk of the population in the two wings of undivided Pakistan. The separatist issues related to language, literature, and politics.

Cultural interchange can bridge many differences – as anyone who in 2006 saw the creation of an image of the Hindu goddess Durga in London's British Museum will attest. In the Great Court of a quintessentially British institution, Bengali craftsmen brought straw, barley, oats, clay, wood and water from the Ganges to create a statue of the goddess. Hundreds of Westerners joined West Bengali Hindus and Bangladeshi Muslims during the five days of Puja and the final immersion of the goddess in the Thames.

As time goes by, the internet is spinning the threads of culture and commerce into the furthest corners of the world, and those threads are stitching and cross-stitching people and communities to each other. How much more difficult will it be to conceive of the world as a small number of hostile camps, assembled under purely religious or cultural banners? As we nurture in ourselves wider global affiliations, we will surely find we share concerns, interests and ideas with people dotted all over the world; and only as we do that will we begin to find that we truly know our own home, our own beginning.

Where, then, is the world heading? Are we heading for a 'flat' world, in which globalization slowly erases the differences between us? Or are we heading for a 'clashing' world of mighty civilizations teetering perilously on the edge of mutual enmity? Neither. Both models are too simplistic. We get nearer to an answer in the complex imagery of Teilhard: we are a world where the globalization of the human presence continues and accelerates, but without reducing individuality. In fact we are becoming *more* distinct and individual, as opposed to communitarian, even as we become ever more irreversibly part of the fabric of global humanity. As we have seen, there is a tension in this paradox, which Teilhard's vision does not and cannot conclusively or unambiguously resolve.

What then *is* globalization? Much of the economic literature and public comment of today is based on the notion that globalization is somehow a concept or an ideology which is the result of conscious decisions. On this reading, globalization is something alien, something that is imposed by governments, or by multinational corporations, or perhaps by Western civilization on the rest of the world.

But, at its most fundamental, the truth is that globalization is not a concept or an ideology: it is a phenomenon. It is part of the sweep of human history. To treat it as something that is being steered by anyone, or any group of people or any group of countries, is to misunderstand what is really happening. Globalization is quite different from the various 'isms' of the last hundred years – communism, fascism, liberalism etc. They really are ideas, and at various times they have had intellectual champions who have sought to make them an accepted basis of political life and government. By contrast, globalization is like population growth. It is a phenomenon that we live with, and that has accelerated very sharply in the past few decades. Governments can – and have – at various times helped or hindered its progress, notably through war and through their policies on trade and capital flows. But, at root, globalization is a phenomenon produced by the human spirit.

The vital point about globalization today is that it has passed the point of no return. We can't pause it, let alone reverse it. This has not always been the case. It wasn't too long ago in the history of humankind that progress could be more or less stopped in its tracks. During the Dark Ages from about AD 500 to AD 700 in western Europe, there was extensive decay. Apart from the scholarship and art that was incubated and preserved in a handful of monasteries, cultural and technological development ground to a halt. Under Roman government, western Europe had experienced stable conditions for trade and manufacture, and a unified cultural and educational system of far-ranging connections. The subsequent steady deterioration of commercial and social linkages and infrastructure resulted in communities becoming increasingly isolated. There was a steep decline in trade and manufacture for export. Major industries, such as pottery, vanished. The crafts of brickmaking and cement-making were lost. Building practically ceased. Administrative and military infrastructures disintegrated and schools collapsed, leading to illiteracy even among the leadership. The number of books plummeted. Organized farming of the land largely vanished, and agricultural yields declined to subsistence level. Meanwhile, of course, the Eastern Empire, with its capital at

Constantinople, continued to flourish. And the Middle East saw the rise of Islam – from inconspicuous beginnings in the Arabian Peninsula – to become a major new civilization which was on its way to becoming the principal centre of learning of the Mediterranean world. The world was still sufficiently *unglobalized* for one region to be effectively closed down while others flourished.

Later on, in the fifteenth century, Ming China too saw a disengagement from the wider world – for different reasons – which resulted in increasing relative weaknesses. A steady growth of Chinese culture and trade had reached its apogee in the opening decades of the fifteenth century. The Ming government was leading world exploration and discovery. It had sponsored seven magnificent exploratory expeditions under the command of the great admiral Zheng He. These expeditions were extraordinary examples of naval skill and power. The fleets visited the Indonesian archipelago, Thailand, India, Arabia and East Africa, and possibly (the records were destroyed) reached beyond the Cape of Good Hope. The first fleet is believed to have consisted of 300 nine-masted treasure ships and 28,000 crew. Wherever Zheng He went, he took a great interest in the local culture. He presented gifts of gold, silver, porcelain and silk; and he brought back samples of his discoveries.

But the expense of these voyages – designed mainly to impress other peoples with the magnificence of Imperial China – was huge. Bureaucratic opposition mounted, and when the emperor who had sponsored Zheng He died, in 1424, the mandarins were able to exert a considerable influence over his son. The result was retrenchment; all overseas trade and contact were cut off. The government abandoned the ships of the fleet, and many captains and admirals were stripped of their rank. China closed its doors on the world overseas. All the court records of Zheng He's voyages were burned. Port facilities were shut down, and seafaring activities were banned. The consequences for Chinese civilization were severe: China's intellectual life gradually became ossified, and the country eventually paid a heavy price in the form of the tragic experiences of the nineteenth and twentieth centuries.

Islam too had its zenith and subsequent decline. During the ninth and tenth centuries Islam had a golden age. While much of Europe was in the grip of paralysis, disease and civil strife, Islamic scientists were inventing algebra and developing geometry, investigating human psychology (they came up with some of the first treatments of mental disorders), and developing the foundations of modern geography (for instance by accurately calculating the circumference and radius of the earth). But from the start of the eleventh century Islam began to apply the brakes on its intellectual life. From around the twelfth century the Islamic world ceased to lead the way in either science or philosophy. The reasons for this stagnation are still debated by historians. Most agree, however, that three significant factors were (i) the savagery of the Mongol invasion of Baghdad in 1258, which overwhelmed the administrative and intellectual heart of Islam (thirty-six libraries were burned down, and the blood of the dead was said to have run as 'high as horses' knees'); (ii) bubonic plague, which hit the Muslim world even harder than Europe, and (iii) the growing religious conservatism of the clerical establishment. For example, the Andalusian polymath Ibn Rushd (known more widely in Europe as Averroës), a man who spanned Eastern and Western traditions and combined a mastery of Islamic philosophy with authorship of many commentaries on the works of Aristotle, was abruptly banished from the Muslim court in Cordoba at the end of the twelfth century because of his perceived excessive rationalism.

And as the world of Islam lost intellectual momentum, Christian Europe surged forward (nourished in part by the fruits of Muslim scholarship) and expanded its power. Its growing intellectual confidence and creative power have their enduring witness in the art, architecture and literature of the high Middle Ages and the Renaissance: this was the era of Milan Cathedral, Dante, the great Renaissance artists, Gutenberg – and exploration.

For all the obvious differences between Ming China and medieval Islam, there is an uncanny parallel between the responses of the Chinese mandarins and the Muslim clerical establishment to the threat of engagement with the outside world. Are these cultural tides related? Did weakness on the part of these two great civilizations create a gap which Europe filled? Possibly. It is certainly a fact that during the axial centuries of the last two thousand years, the renaissance of Europe was going on broadly at the same as the closing of the borders in China and the loss of traction in the Islamic world. It is likely that Europe's increasing strength was facilitated, in part at least, by the increasing weakness of both China and Islam, and that this rebalancing of the world's civilizations helped drive Europe to create the foundations of the modern world. Consider the world in 1492. It was the year of the fall of Granada and the final extinction of Muslim Spain, and just a few years after the burning of Zheng He's records in the Chinese imperial court. But it was also the year when Christopher Columbus sailed from Spain to the New World, starting a voyage of discovery which led to the Europeanization of the Americas.

If it takes the closing down of some parts of the global system for another part to dominate, then the like of this will probably never happen again. Barring some huge cataclysm, we are all now in the same torrent of progress, and we are all going to be carried along by it at an increasingly similar pace. We will not see whole civilizations turn in on themselves and wither. It is increasingly impossible to be culturally isolationist. The exceptions today are relatively tiny parts of the world that, for a while, are forced by doctrinaire and fanatical leaderships to be hermetically sealed from progress at the price of immense human suffering. Even in these cases, the enforced darkness may last a generation or two, but eventually release will come. In the Middle Ages the world was not sufficiently interconnected for an intellectual and economic vacuum in one region to be filled from elsewhere. Such a vacuum cannot persist on any significant scale in the twenty-first century. It is not possible for whole regions to remain isolated from the world's accumulated knowledge.

Where, then, will globalization lead us? Over the next fifty years, its main political impact will be to create a more multipolar world. But it will also change societies, urbanizing them and individualizing them. It will bring with it a new burst of cultural interaction and creativity. And commercial connectedness and exchange will become ever more intense.

A more multipolar world is already upon us. This is, in fact, not so much a new chapter in the history of the world as a reversion to the historical norm. Only twice in history has there been a single global superpower. First, the British Empire from 1815 to (arguably) the unification of Germany in 1871. And, second, the US supremacy from the fall of the Berlin Wall in 1989 to . . . around now.

There was no unipolar period in history before 1815. The Roman Empire and the Chinese Han Empire governed roughly the same number of people (around 60 million). Though they coexisted for some 250 years, they had little if any contact with each other; they never clashed, or recorded each other's triumphs. If only they had. The Romans could have shown off their new discovery, glass, at much the same time as the Chinese could have shown off theirs, porcelain. In many other ways – scientific, literary, architectural – the two civilizations marched in (unconscious) step. However, in many respects, China was well ahead of Europe in technical invention. Chinese scientists developed the first paper, discovered how to forge steel, produced the first seismometer, correctly discovered that the moon was reflecting the light of the sun, and designed the first winnowing machine for farmers. Europe, on the other hand, benefited from alphabetic script – the concept of which was first developed in Mesopotamia in the second millennium BC – which China never adopted. Philosophy, literature and art flourished in both civilizations, and roads (now referred to as the silk routes) were opened up to allow trade across the Eurasian land mass. It was a world that was, at the very least, bipolar.

Nor was the world unipolar at the time of the Mongol Empire, which numbered a massive 110 million people by the thirteenth century. The Mongols had a devastating impact on Islam, and were a major threat to both China and a nascent Russia, but had little impact on the affairs of Western Christendom. Nor did the Spanish Empire represent a unipolar moment. In 1600 it numbered around 60 million people, and seemed to Europeans to dominate the world. But the Ming Empire at the same time numbered around 150 million people, and, sealed from the rest of the world, Ming civilization was scarcely impacted by the Spanish at all.

It was only after the fall of Napoleonic France, in 1815, that Britain, because of its dominance of the sea, became the first country in the history of the world to establish an empire that had no rival and had global reach. It eventually became the biggest empire ever in terms of population (over 500 million). It could afford to go to almost any lengths to remove awkward political customers – as evidenced famously by the 1868 expedition to Abyssinia to rescue two hostages from imprisonment by the Ethiopian emperor Tewodros. The British government considered it an affair of honour, and dispatched General Sir Robert Napier with an army of 13,000 soldiers and a supporting group of 26,000 camp followers, 40,000 animals (including elephants) and 280 ships. After a long, hot journey the final battle took under two hours, the British lost one man, the Ethiopians 700, the hostages were released, and the Emperor committed suicide.

Politically, there was no other power that could seriously hamper British rule until 1871, when the Prussian chief minister Otto von Bismarck managed to unify a number of independent German states into a nation state and thus create the German Empire. The geo-political force that thus came into being was a phenomenal success, releasing an immediate wave of patriotism and economic growth. In 1871 there were 41 million citizens in Germany. Thirty years later there were around 60 million. During that same period, German steel production multiplied by twelve, coal production multiplied by five, and exports tripled. By 1914 Germany was the most powerful industrial nation in the world. The years of British supremacy were clearly over.

The second period in which the world has had a clear single global superpower began with the last throes of the Cold War, in 1989. It was widely assumed that the end of the old Soviet/US bipolar world would usher in a multipolar structure, with power dispersed to new centres such as Japan, Germany and China. It didn't happen. The US became the sole superpower. The American newspaper columnist Charles Krauthammer could confidently declare in a Washington lecture delivered in September 1990, 'Now is the unipolar moment. There is today no lack of second-rank powers. Germany and Japan are economic dynamos. Britain and France can deploy diplomatic and to some extent military assets. The Soviet Union possesses several elements of power – military, diplomatic and political – but all are in rapid decline. There is but one first-rate power and no prospect in the immediate future of any power to rival it.'

It will have lasted no more than about a generation. In 2004 the National Intelligence Council, the leading US intelligence organization, was predicting 'continued US dominance', adding that 'most major powers have forsaken the idea of balancing the US.' But in 2008 its four-yearly global-trends review had a very different story to tell. It concluded that the world was entering an unstable and unpredictable period in which the advance of Western democracy could not be taken for granted and the US would no longer be able to 'call the shots' alone. It predicted a decline of EU influence and a sharp rise in the influence of emerging economies such as Brazil, India and China. International relations were reverting to type: a multipolar world was coming into being again.

The re-emergence of China as a world power is the most important event of the first half of this century. It will be described by many as the 'emergence' of China, but in fact we should not forget that it is a return to a lengthy status quo ante – for eighteen of the past twenty centuries China has been the world's largest economy. *The Economist* not long ago described it thus: 'China was not only the largest economy for much of recorded history, but until the fifteenth century, it also had the highest income *per capita* – and was the world's technological leader.' As recently as 1820, China accounted for one-third of the world's GDP while the US accounted for a mere 2 per cent. By 1914 the tables had turned, with the US accounting for 19 per cent of global GDP and China, which had been almost completely bypassed by the European Industrial Revolution of the nineteenth century, less than 10 per cent. But the pattern is changing again: China is returning to the world stage. Since its own internal free-market reforms, in 1978, China's GDP has grown at an average of around 10 per cent a year. Today China is the fastest growing economy in the world, and within twenty years, by many predictions, it will (once again) be the largest.

So a more multipolar world is dawning, and the political currents that will guide it are already flowing. The phenomenon of globalization, however, is not simply a matter of international political relationships. It is also having a profound effect on human society everywhere, whatever the political form of governance – democratic or otherwise. Almost everywhere, people are becoming more urbanized and more individualized. The process is largely driven in the less economically developed countries by lack of resources in rural areas and the (oft-misguided) lure of higher standards of living in the cities. At the last count, in 2008, there were 473 cities in the world with over 1 million inhabitants. The number has nearly doubled in under twenty years. In 1850 there were probably just three: London, Paris and Beijing.

This breathless rate of change has helped dismantle many of the old communitarian and social structures. The causal link between urbanization and individualization is profound and virtually universal, even though the pace and extent of individualization clearly vary among the different cultures of the world. Europeans are probably in the vanguard. In Europe, all sorts of structures that were taken for granted as part of the social fabric half a century ago are in decline. In Britain, for example, Churches, working men's associations, Masons, Boy Scouts, the Women's Institute and many other smaller and more local organizations that held society together have shrunk in size and influence, whereas only fifty years ago they were established features of the British social landscape and were taken as much for granted as the daily milk delivery and the sight of the policeman on his bicycle.

The US is very different: though the degree of urbanization is similar (at the turn of the century, three out of four Americans and roughly the same proportion of Europeans lived in urban areas), and both are prosperous, America's patriotism, religiousness and sense of common purpose stand in striking contrast to a Europe which can sometimes – even to Europeans themselves – seem to lack both compass and anchor. The fact is that Europeans have become more secularized than Americans, more children of the eighteenth-century Enlightenment; and this secularization – in a post-fascist, post-communist age – is accompanied by a degree of individualization which impacts almost all aspects of life and more extensively than in any other culture today. It is hard to think of anywhere else in the world with a comparable philosophical outlook – with what is, in some ways, one notable (and perhaps surprising) exception: China.

The distinguishing feature of Chinese civilization is that China is the only society where there has never been a deep-rooted theistic religion at the centre of the culture. It is not that the Chinese weren't religious, but from a very early stage Chinese thought was funda-mentally deistic. It has no specific creation story, and revelation, miracles and mysticism generally were shunned. Chinese philosophy was highly attractive to some European Enlightenment scholars. Sir William Temple – seventeenth-century English diplomat, and a fairly typical Enlightenment spokesman – energetically enthused about Confucius, proclaiming at one stage that Confucius's 'chief principle' was that everyone ought to 'study and endeavour the improving and perfecting of his own natural reason to the greatest height he is capable' and claiming him as an Enlightenment hero.

The comparison can be overdrawn, of course. Chinese culture has a strongly superstitious streak (although this characteristic of popular belief should not be underestimated in secularized Europe either). And it would be a serious mistake to overlook the strength and cohesiveness of Chinese patriotism (in which China resembles America much more than it does Europe). Nevertheless, it is arguable that Europe and China are now the two most secularized civiliza-tions in the world. The Confucian ethos has given China a rationalist pragmatism as a basis for the values of life and a social psychology which is by instinct well attuned to individualized urban existence. (This is not, of course, to argue that crowd psychology and hysteria cannot take over in times of social and political stress – as evidenced in Europe in the 1930s and China in the 1960s. But in both cases these were deviations from an underlying rational pragmatism.)

Is the rest of Asia fundamentally different in the way it is being affected by urbanization and globalization? Certainly not the other Asian giant, India. In 2006 the editor of *Newsweek International*, Fareed Zakaria, described the explosion of post-globalization economic and cultural energy in India as going far beyond the economic statistics. 'Indians, at least in urban areas, are bursting with enthusiasm. Indian businessmen are giddy about their prospects. Indian designers and artists speak of extending their influence across the globe. Bollywood movie stars want to grow their audience abroad from their "base" of half a billion fans. It is as if hundreds of millions of people have suddenly discovered the keys to unlock their potential.'

If there is any lasting Asian exception to the individualizing effects of urbanization, it may well be Japan. Highly urbanized, prosperous, and extensively open to Western trade and travel, Japan has nonetheless largely defied the sweeping progress of individualization. In a 2008 article for the *Financial Times*, the Tokyo bureau chief David Pilling meditated at length on his belief that there is no such thing as Japanese exceptionalism and that 'people are people and that any attempt to render them otherwise probably has an ulterior motive'. He worked hard to prove the thesis, interviewing first one expert and then another. But in the end he acknowledged that it had to remain unproven. All the scholars that he consulted came down on the side of Japan's impenetrable difference. In fact Cambridge anthropologist Alan Macfarlane contends that Japan is not just 'trivially different from the West and other civilizations, but different at such a deep level that the very tools of understanding we normally use prove inadequate'. No other big country has spent so much of its history largely isolated by the sea from contact with the rest of the world. It is not just that Japan's separateness is exaggerated by the fact that it is the only Buddhist-rooted society to join the rich man's club of the Group of Seven, which is otherwise culturally monotheistic-Christian. Macfarlane bases his view partly on the fact that Japan has never gone through the Aristotelian (or indeed Confucian) process of separating the world of matter from the world of spirit. Pilling asked Akira Chiba, a successful diplomat, how he conceived of God, and get the reply, 'In Japan, gods are floating all around.

Essentially, we live together with the gods.' Pilling quoted a book that describes Europeans and Americans (and, he might have added, the Chinese) as being like eggs with their own protective shell. 'The Japanese, by contrast, were shell-less, unable to conceive of themselves other than in relation to family, village, workplace, superiors and inferiors, insiders and outsiders.'

And what about the Islamic world? There the culture is in many areas profoundly religious in its ethos in a way which ceased to be the case in Europe from the eighteenth century and in a way that China has never been. How will this civilization be affected by urbanization (which is spreading in Muslim countries as fast as anywhere else)? All the evidence is that the impact is and will be profound. It is worth noting, for example, that fertility rates are declining under the impact of urbanization (and female education) virtually everywhere. In Muslim countries as diverse as Turkey, Iran, Algeria and Indonesia (and their obvious diversity sends a warning about the dangers of oversimplistic characterization of countries in terms of culture), fertility is now down at, or close to, replacement levels.

In the world of ideas – both literary and scientific or technical – the memory of the extraordinary creativity that characterized Muslim civilization in past centuries has never disappeared. There is a clear recognition among a wide range of Muslim thinkers that there is ground to be made up. The evidence lies, for example, in a 2003 United Nations study written by Arab social scientists, which calculated that the Arabic world at the turn of the century produced 1.1 per cent of the world's books with 5 per cent of the population and in 1998 all the Arab countries combined produced fewer literary and artistic books than Turkey (with one-quarter of the population). But today all this is beginning to change. And of course parts of the Muslim world now have substantial resources to invest in supporting a renaissance. In publishing, for example, there have recently been new initiatives like Kaleem Books, launched out of the UAE with the following bold marketing proclamation: 'In the twentieth century the Arabic-speaking world experienced a reawakening of literary freedom and zeal that continues to flourish and pick up momentum.

This revitalization of creative and passionate expression is captured in Kaleem Books – its authors and readers alike comprise the next generation of enlightened Arabic-speaking literati across the Arab world – and across the globe.'

Overall, there is simply no reason to believe that Islamic society will be unchanged by urbanization and by the connectedness and individualization that is intrinsic to it. Even in Saudi Arabia, the powerful theocratic kingdom which is guardian to the Muslim holy cities of Mecca and Medina, Khalid al-Faisal, one of the leading members of the ruling royal family, himself governor of the province of Mecca, could commission a 2009 relaunch of his national newspaper *Al-Watan* with the avowed intention of advancing openness inside the country.

Overall, the trend is clear, and there will be few enduring exceptions. These great changes in international relationships and in society all over the world have huge implications and present obvious challenges which will be explored more fully in later chapters. Connectedness and individualization – the twin focuses of Teilhard de Chardin's vision of human development – are increasing everywhere. This is not just a phenomenon of commerce and economics: it is something far more profound, which reaches deep into the roots of human self-definition. And one of its most exciting and creative manifestations is in the realm of cultural exchange. Anyone who travels today cannot fail to note the rapidly accelerating interplay of cultural ideas and inspiration around an increasingly globalized world.

The Qatar Museum of Islamic Art opened in November 2008, offering a rich display of treasures from Islamic culture throughout the world, amid signs of an intent to invest in collecting treasures from other cultures too. If this vision is followed through, the result could eventually be to assemble collections as varied in their reflection of human creativity as those in Berlin, London, New York and Paris.

In Beijing, the 798 Space located in the Dashanzi area, to the north-east of central Beijing, is the site of several former state-owned factories including Factory 798, which originally produced electronic goods. However, from around 2002 artists and cultural organizations began to rent and remake the factory spaces, gradually developing them into a hive of arts and crafts. As you walk around, the energy and inventiveness are palpable. It is an exciting place. And some of what makes it exciting is to do with the extraordinary mix of cultures that are at work there. Chinese revolutionary motifs sit beside traditional Chinese art and modern innovative Chinese design influenced by, but not slavishly imitating, Western and Japanese themes. It seems like a micro-system of global cultures.

At the 2007 Beijing Music Festival the young Chinese pianist Lang Lang played Brahms's First Piano Concerto to an audience drawn from the Beijing establishment. The power of this deeply Romantic nineteenth-century German music transfixed the auditorium, and effortlessly bridged – but without eliminating – the cultural gulf between two civilizations firmly rooted in their respective sense of the power of the aesthetic. Similarly, I have listened to the work of an Italian composer (Puccini) in a Chinese opera house (in Beijing) designed by a Frenchman (Paul Andreu). Puccini's final work is based on a classic and well-loved Chinese opera story (*Turandot*), and his music in that opera seamlessly synthesizes European and Chinese tonality. For this performance, a new ending had been commissioned from a young composer at Beijing's Central Conservatory, Hao Weiya.* The staging, by Gao Guangjian, echoed the grandeur of the real imperial palace across the street from the opera house, and drew on the typical motifs of Chinese opera. The production held its audience spellbound.

And the world's cultural exchange is becoming ever more multi-faceted and multidirectional. Europe and America in recent years have seen a growing number of globally diverse exhibitions, concerts and literature. In 2008 the Victoria & Albert Museum in London mounted an important exhibition of modern Chinese design (China Design Now), while in 2009 the Saatchi Gallery in Chelsea mounted

---

*Puccini died leaving *Turandot* unfinished, with the clues to what he intended sketched on 23 sheets of manuscript paper. The commonly performed ending is by a contemporary, Franco Alfano. Hao Weiya's new ending is based on 'Jasmine Flower', a traditional Chinese folk song.

45

an exhibition of work from the Levant and the Middle East – the creations of young Muslim artists seeking, through the lens of modern urban life, to interpret in art their Muslim culture, its aesthetics and its human relationships.

And this story of cultural exchange is becoming more and more widespread. Indian sculpture from the third century, exquisite in its detail, has travelled westward; as have paintings done in Jodhpur over two hundred years ago which, for their use of colour as a gateway to mystery, might be said to anticipate Rothko. There have been huge numbers of new English translations of literary works from Asia, Africa, the Middle East and Latin America. Not all of this will endure. Some cultural exchange is fed by novelty and fashion. But this is not trivial dumbing down towards some lowest common denominator. It is an interaction that leads to creative enrichment, just as previous cultural intersections in earlier centuries sparked new inspiration (Gauguin and Tahiti, Van Gogh and Japanese painting, Picasso and African art, and so on).

So the impact of globalization is multifaceted. Shifting balances of power, urbanization, individualization and cultural interaction are all caused by the phenomenon (not the ideology) that has, like it or not, come to define our age.

In one sense, the *least* interesting aspect of globalization is commerce, even though it is commerce which lies at its root. Odysseus is often held up by classical scholars as the archetypal combination of the inquisitive and acquisitive explorer. When he goes into the huge cave which is the home of the monster Polyphemus, at least part of his motive for ignoring his companions' sensible advice and entering the trap is to see if he can swap gifts with the monster and take something interesting home with him. The rest of his motive is simply to have a look. Like Odysseus, humanity at large is still burdened with the inquisitive/acquisitive urge in equal measure. In one sense, the story of humanity is the story of those who journey far from home: Xuanzang, Marco Polo, Zheng He, Ibn Battuta, Magellan, Columbus. We push out from our home base and search for excitement, not just profit, not necessarily knowing what we are looking for, or even what we have found. Globalization is about far more than commerce, even if the impetus behind it is trade.

This is all interconnected. Connected commerce is what causes the rise of cities. Cities are what gradually individualize us and connect us culturally. And that poses the question of who we are (which the art that flourishes through cultural exchange strives one way or another to answer).

So now we need to look at the global bazaar.

3

The Global Bazaar

*Money . . . is the oil which renders the motion of the wheels
[of trade] more smooth and easy.*
David Hume, *Essays Moral and Political* (1741)

Money speaks sense in a language all nations understand.
Aphra Behn, *The Rover* (1681)

The love of money is the root of all evil.
St Paul, First Letter to Timothy

The beginnings of globalization lie in the beginnings of humanity.
Yet the phenomenon was not defined or discussed until late in the
nineteenth century, about a century before the word itself became
common currency. This, for example, was written in the US in 1897
(with the patronizing tone characteristic of the time):

The civilized peoples are no longer strangers in any part of the earth.
Their splendid sea equipments carry their business representatives, their
political envoys and their curious pleasure-seekers to the remotest quarters
with ease and comfort. Magnificent railway coaches introduce them to the
interior lands, and they return home laden with information, and with
new ideas, and awakened to new projects and enterprises. Even the
dull heathen nations are arousing themselves from the dreams of centuries
and looking with wonder and amazement at their visitors from abroad
and learning of their marvellous achievements. And they in turn are now

sending their representatives abroad that they may profit by their new acquaintances.

The author was a 45-year-old Protestant evangelist, Charles Taze Russell. His experience and interests were a lively mixture of commerce and religion. At the tender age of 12, when he wasn't chalking Bible verses on the pavement to convert the heathen, he was encouraged to run some of his father's Pittsburgh clothes stores and write business contracts for customers. The young merchant went on to become a noted writer and religious leader, eccentric in some ways and visionary in others. As well as his intimations of globalization, Russell believed that the world would see a significant but gradual change in the earth's climate, including the gradual melting of the polar ice caps. This early prophet of globalization was perhaps also the first prophet of global warming, but long before either notion became familiar.

It was not until eighty-six years later, in 1983, that the word 'globalization' itself was popularized. In 'The Globalization of Markets', an essay in the *Harvard Business Review*, the iconoclastic marketing theorist and Harvard Business School professor Theodore Levitt launched a thesis that caused a storm of controversy. He proclaimed that new technologies had 'proletarianized' communications, transport and travel, creating a new commercial reality – the emergence of global markets for standardized consumer products at lower prices, thanks to economies of scale. He described a sea change in manufacturing that was especially advantageous to companies such as Coca-Cola, Kellogg's and McDonald's. He went further still and argued that multinational corporations would evolve into 'global corporations' that did not need to cater to local differences in taste. When he died, in 2006, the *New York Times*, in its obituary, gave Levitt credit for coining the word 'globalization' – only to have to make hasty retractions as evidence to the contrary flooded in, including examples from as early as 1944 in non-economic senses, and in economics from several years before publication of Levitt's essay.

In fact the true origins of globalization lie in the roots of human behaviour and in the mists of time. Both Thomas Friedman and

Teilhard de Chardin in their different ways have written eloquently about the way that globalization emerges from the deepest instincts of humanity. For Friedman, writing in 1999 in his book *The Lexus and the Olive Tree*, globalization had a quasi-religious value. It could, he said, heal two of the deepest human yearnings: the desire for 'sustenance, improvement, prosperity and modernization' (the Lexus) and the longing for 'everything that roots us, anchors us, identifies us and locates us in this world' (the olive tree). We need to satisfy both desires, he argued. Governments can facilitate our drive towards the Lexus, but we have to create our own paths to our own olive tree. For Teilhard de Chardin, writing half a century earlier, globalization was the deep-rooted religious movement of his age. He connected it to the mystics' desire for oneness with the infinite, to what he called the Omega Point. And he used the vocabulary of mysticism to describe global developments in technology, industry, politics, and the environment. But the roots of the phenomenon were in evolution and humanity's gradual spread across the face of the globe.

The interactive digital map The Journey of Mankind, created by the Bradshaw Foundation, graphically tells the story. Anyone who wishes to see it can find it today via Google. With the first click of a mouse, a red dot appears in East Africa marking the region where, from approximately 160,000 years ago, the earliest known archaeological traces of *Homo sapiens* have been found. Over the next thirty-five thousand years, groups of hunter-gatherers set forth to explore the limits of their world; the red lines of their journeyings stretch south and south-west and west to the edges of the continent. The first exit from Africa, north across the Sahara and up the Nile, comes to a stop during a global cooling in around 100,000 BC. The second exit, ten thousand years later, across the mouth of the Red Sea and along the south coast of the Arabian Peninsula, is more successful. All non-African people are descended from those who made this journey. Only ten thousand years later, humanity has snaked a winding path around India and Indonesia to South China. The eruption of Mount Toba in Sumatra causes a thousand-year Ice Age and a dramatic population crash. But by 25,000 BC the Eurasian land mass is populated from the west to the far north-east, resulting in the next great migration, following the big game herds across the Bering land bridge connecting Siberia to Alaska and down into North America – the first, but not the last, migration into the Americas. The final Ice Age stops progress for another few thousand years, but by around 12,500 BC the lines have reached all over the globe – to the southern tip of America, to Australia, and north to the Arctic.

Teilhard's vision of humanity spreading over the surface of the sphere of the earth is brought to life on the map as the lines of human exploration slowly stretch away from each other until they meet again. And, however vulnerable people were to disease, famine and natural disaster, it is clear that even in 12,500 BC a process had started that would be unstoppable. Within the next five thousand years the first known pottery was being used in Japan. And from that era too archaeologists have found traces of the first domesticated wheat: humanity's staple food, and the crop which more than any other (including rice or maize) has supported the growth in the earth's population from less than 10 million to more than 6 billion over the past ten thousand years. It had taken *Homo sapiens* 150,000 years to spread out over the planet and lay down the beginnings of a safer, more sustainable life. The human adventure had started slowly. But over the next 10,000 years it dramatically speeded up.

Much of the known history of humanity is the story of migration. *Homo sapiens* was driven by an urge to keep exploring for more fertile land and better food – though often the search led not just to health and prosperity, but to competition and conflict. Of the earliest recorded migrations, one of the most fascinating is the spread of the Aryans, now generally believed to be the original ancestors of all the Indo-European peoples in the world. And, continuously down the ages, migration has shaped and reshaped the cultural and political geography of the planet. From the Celts to the Angles and Saxons, the Huns, the Vikings, the Magyars, the Turks and the Mongols, and the Yayoi who crossed into Japan via the Korean Peninsula, one way or another humanity wove its tapestry over the earth, gathering and splitting, twining and joining. And in the course of this arose a yet more powerful engine of globalization: trade.

Adam Smith thought that human nature had an inbuilt propensity to 'truck, barter, and exchange one thing for another'. Evolutionary anthropology shows that he was right. Animals share food and groom each other, protect their young, create social structures, and move in groups; but only *Homo sapiens* has developed a systematic exchange of goods and services. When humans in the Fertile Crescent of Mesopotamia, Assyria and Phoenicia first began to create gadgets and knick-knacks that other humans envied – for instance, carved bone antler tools and the atlatl (a throwing stick that hugely improved on the range and accuracy of the spear) – paleoanthropologists surmise that the first communications and exchanges were taking place. Later, northern European Stone Age humans invented boats for hunting and used them to transport heavy game; once they had transport and communication skills, they had the means to trade.

One of the earliest commodities traded by boat was the black volcanic glass called obsidian, which was easily chipped into cutting tools and weapons. Flakes twelve thousand years old found in mainland Greece have been traced back to the volcano on the island of Melos, a hundred miles offshore. By 3000 BC, Sumerian farmers were trading their grain for copper, obtained hundreds of miles west in the Sinai Desert. This was the typical pattern of early trade – the exchange of grain from farmers living in river valleys for metals from herders living in the hills. And, inevitably, it wasn't long before trading itself became a specialized activity.

By 1000 BC the world had its first trading professionals. The rise of the Red Sea trade route as a commercial artery to rival and eclipse the Persian Gulf followed the westward spread of civilization from the Euphrates into Egypt and Greece. This new route was dominated and run by the Phoenicians, who had settled in what is now Lebanon. Sitting in the middle of the Fertile Crescent in a land richly forested with suitable boat-building timber, the Phoenicians enjoyed unparalleled strategic and natural advantages. When the Bible's first

Book of Kings records Solomon fetching huge quantities of gold from Ophir (possibly in the Indian subcontinent), it was transported by the navy of Hiram. Hiram was the king of Tyre, the dominant Phoenician city. From around 900 BC, Phoenicians established colonies throughout the Mediterranean: their Canaanite gods were worshipped from Cyprus to Sardinia, Malta, Sicily, Iberia and Carthage. They were the greatest navigators of their era, skilled at night sailing using the 'Phoenician star' (the pole star). Their wallowing, bathtub-shaped merchant ships were huge. Using square sails and oars when the wind dropped, they could probably carry loads of over 400 tons. By 400 BC, it is believed, the Phoenicians were regularly navigating most of the western European coastline as well as the coasts of both western and eastern Africa. And with increasing travelling distances came increased access to rare goods that entranced and dazzled the rulers of the ancient world.

The mere fact that a commodity came from a distant land imbued it with status. In his 2008 book *A Splendid Exchange – How Trade Shaped the World*, the financial historian William J. Bernstein illustrates the point with the story of Chinese silk in the third century AD. The Roman aristocracy went wild for it. The majority of European clothing at the time was made from animal skins or wool. Skins were heavy, and wool was rough. The arrival of an alternative that was cheaper than cotton (hard to produce and prohibitively expensive), light, soft and adaptable to almost any colour, and comfortable to wear, electrified wealthy Romans. Yet they knew nothing of China. They believed that silk grew directly on the mulberry tree. Trading distances were vast enough to necessitate a multi-stage journey. During the third century, most silk came to Europe from China by sea to Sri Lanka. Indian merchants would then take the cargo to mainland India. Then Greek and Arab traders would sail it to the (now Yemeni) island of Socotra; there it would be transferred to Greek ships that would carry it through the Red Sea to Egypt, to be taken by camel across the desert to the Nile. For the final stage, it would be picked up from Alexandria by Italian ships for transit to cargo ports such as Ostia, near Rome. The Chinese scarcely ever went further than Sri Lanka. At each stage of the journey, information would certainly be watered down. Fabulous, rare and unimaginably hard to find – luxury was ever marketed thus.

And never more so than in the trade in exotic spices. The world's most sought-after commodities in the European Middle Ages were cinnamon, nutmeg, mace and cloves. Their supply lines were the commercial links of the early world. Their profits funded some of the wonders of the world – for example, the public architecture of Venice was built largely on the profits from spice trading. The rarity value of these commodities was huge, and they became status symbols as much because of their expense and mystery as because of their flavour. Cloves grew only on five tiny islands in the North Moluccas in what is now eastern Indonesia. Nutmeg and mace grew only on nine tiny islands in the South Moluccas. Cinnamon came from Sri Lanka, just on the edge of what for Europeans was the known world. At the height of its popularity, cinnamon flower juice was valued weight for weight the same as gold. For nearly a thousand years after nutmeg, mace and cloves first appeared in Europe their source was unknown to consumers. The three trading routes – the Red Sea, the Persian Gulf and the Silk Road – were beyond the control of the European merchant states, in the hands of Muslim traders.

Not all spices were top-end luxuries, however. The larger merchant ships needed ballast, and one type of ballast that the merchants could always sell was pepper from the Western Ghats, the mountain range strung along India's Malabar Coast. Pepper was universally in demand throughout ancient Europe to garnish the porridge-like Roman diet of boiled barley and wheat. It became an instant success, both with Romans throughout the empire and with their various barbarian aggressors. (Alaric the Goth was said to be a particular aficionado.)

Pepper was in use in far-flung corners of Europe such as the British Isles from at least the fifth century. When the Hoxne Hoard was discovered in Suffolk in 1992, it was the richest find of Roman treasure yet unearthed in Britain. The day after its discovery it was taken to the British Museum. Once cleaned up, resplendent among the fifteen thousand coins were four silver pepper pots or *piperatoria*.

The finest of them is a hollow bust of an imperial lady of the late-Roman period. Details of the empress's jewellery and rich clothing are gilded, and she holds a scroll in her left hand. The pot has a disc in the base which could be turned to three positions: one closed, one with large openings to enable the pot to be filled with ground pepper, and a third with small holes for sprinkling. The owner would have been a powerful and privileged Roman, but the contents of the silver pot would have been known more widely. And as time went by it was the broader population whose needs would eventually begin to exert their influence ever more powerfully on trade, and to globalize it.

In the wake of the great voyages of discovery of the fifteenth and sixteenth centuries and the discovery of the New World by the Old, the worldwide expansion of the global economy really began. The Americas opened the way to new riches for Europe. Among other commodities, vast supplies of gold and silver were unlocked. 'Get gold, humanely if you can; but at all hazards, get gold!' wrote Spain's King Ferdinand to his New World colonists in 1511. It didn't take long. New supplies of gold and silver began flowing east across the Atlantic from 1513, when Balboa annexed the Panama isthmus for Spain; from 1519, when Cortés conquered Mexico; and from 1531–4, when Pizarro encountered and overthrew the Inca Empire. Beginning in 1531 and over the following forty-year period, Peruvian bullion shipped to Spain was something like 100 million pieces of gold, and twice as much in silver. And it was this influx of bullion from the New World that gave Europe its next big jolt and set the wheels turning in a direction that would eventually lay the foundations of today's modern globalized economy.

Over the next 150 years, from the early sixteenth century to the middle of the seventeenth, there was a price revolution across western Europe. Inflation was rampant, driving up prices by an average of six times. What lay behind this? First, and chiefly, the massive flow of bullion from the Spanish treasure fleet: there was simply too much money for the amount of available goods. But patterns of supply and demand were also changing at the same time. In both agriculture and crafts there was an increase in production for the market rather than just for subsistence, as new markets were created through trade. But trade communication lines were fragile and easily disrupted, with the result that shortages and interruptions in the supply chain could have a sharp effect on prices. There were demographic forces at work too: the slow but steady rise in the size of Europe's population (increasingly living in towns) meant there were more people to feed. Food production struggled to keep up, and prices tended to rise.

The effect of sustained inflation on Europe was profound. Inflation tended to redistribute wealth up the social chain to the owners of land. Moreover, European merchants were beginning to supplant Arab and Indian traders in East Asia and were becoming prosperous. In many a trading town the quality of life leaped sharply. For the first time the new middle classes had money for discretionary spending and time in which to enjoy it. Among other effects, the extraordinary profusion of Dutch and Flemish art of this period is evidence of what was under way.

All of which drove demand for the new luxuries of life: sugar and cotton. Sugar, which Bernstein calls 'the heroin of foodstuffs', was widely addictive, and demand hugely exceeded supply. The average per capita consumption in Europe in the fifteenth century had been around one teaspoon per year. From the sixteenth century the demand for sugar exploded. (Today the teaspoon has become a wheelbarrow, with European per-capita annual sugar consumption sitting at over 36 kg.) The problem was finding a suitably warm climate for sugar cane. The tropics of the New World provided it. During the lifetime of Columbus, the cultivation of sugar cane spread rapidly from southern China, Indochina and India to Central America. The sugar belt soon reached from Brazil to Surinam and across the Caribbean to Cuba, touching off a commercial explosion that powered much of the world economy for the next three centuries.

Cotton evolved very rapidly into a major trade commodity soon after. Up until about 1600 cotton was a luxury product on a par with silk. By the 1650s it became a commercial plantation crop, and Barbados became the first colony to export it. By the 1840s India was no longer capable of supplying the vast quantities of cotton needed by British factories, and the supply moved decisively to America. In deference to its economic power, it came to be known as 'King Cotton' – and by the mid nineteenth century it had become the mainstay of the commercial life of the southern United States.

By the mid nineteenth century, trade – with Europe at its hub – had become a high-volume business. From tentative beginnings in obsidian, copper and tin, through luxury imports of spice and silk, to a more inclusive traffic in sugar and cotton, the idea and practice of commerce had taken their first, sometimes faltering, steps on the global stage. In the 190 years between the launch of the first proper European banknotes in 1661 by Stockholms Banco, a predecessor of the Swedish central bank, and the 1851 Great Exhibition in London, trade came of age. It would never look back. By the year of the Great Exhibition, the world's first industrial society (Britain) was teetering on the brink of mass-market consumerism. From the Manchester slums in the 1850s to the consumer world of the car, domestic appliances, fresh food from every climate all year round, digital cameras and a wardrobe full of machine-made clothes from around the world is a journey of only a century and a half.

What accounts for the astonishing speed of progress? It is a confluence of three developments in particular: first, wholesale movements of people; second, a stream of new inventions which powered the Industrial Revolution; and, third, trade. In the nineteenth century they became interrelated and mutually reinforcing, leading to large increases in supply, demand and trade across a widening spectrum of goods and over a swiftly growing proportion of the earth's surface.

The nineteenth century saw huge movements of people within countries, caused by urbanization. Britain set the pace, and set the pattern for urbanization elsewhere – a trend which continues today in the world's developing economies. The Industrial Revolution, which moved work from small-scale cottage industries to large-scale factories employing thousands of workers with very little access to public or private transport, meant that people had to live close to the factories. The fastest-growing towns and cities were located in areas with easy access to water and/or coal. In the decades leading up to 1850, there was rapid change in the relative significance of different cities as a consequence. Industrialization lifted new towns like Birmingham to prominence, and older county towns such as Chester and Exeter lost their relative importance. And from the mid nineteenth century Britain's urban hierarchy was set, dominated by major manufacturing centres and ports. It has changed little since.

The numbers tell the story. In 1801, at the time of the first UK census, only about 20 per cent of the population lived in towns. By 1851 the figure had risen to over 50 per cent, and by 1881 to around 75 per cent. The major cities in 1851 were London (with 2.6 million inhabitants) and Glasgow, Liverpool, Manchester and Birmingham (with populations of around 350,000). By 1900 London had over 6 million inhabitants, and the four big regional cities had over 500,000 each. Overall, in the forty years between 1851 and 1891 the urban population of England and Wales more than doubled – from just under 10 million to nearly 22 million. Large numbers of people had been uprooted from their farms and villages and moved to the new manufacturing hubs of an increasingly mechanized and powerful economy – often into slums scarcely better than the favellas of today's emerging markets.

The newly globalized world of the eighteenth and nineteenth centuries also saw an even grimmer phenomenon. For the second major movement of people around this time was the slave trade. Both sugar-cane and cotton production in the New World depended on a sure supply of labour which could be made to work in brutal conditions. The solution was the commercialization of slavery. The African slave trade was old: at least a four-hundred-year story of forcible transportation under unspeakable circumstances. It was the only significant forced mass migration in history (though there have of course been other forced *expulsions*). How many Africans were shipped to the New World? Today the generally received figure is between 10 and 12 million. Whatever the exact total, it is broadly agreed that the trade reached its climax in the last hundred years before it was abolished, and that between 1750 and 1850 some

7 million Africans were forcibly transported across the Atlantic – a number equivalent, in 1850, to around half the population of England. It remains one of the greatest moral crimes in the whole of human history.

Then the nineteenth century saw a third great movement of people: the transatlantic migration of European peasants and labourers to the New World. Encouraged by vastly improved transport, and unable to find work in the cities of their home countries, around 55 million people moved from Europe to the Americas between 1846 and 1940, two-thirds of them to the USA. (Other major destinations were Argentina, Canada, Brazil and Cuba.) Many of the Europeans – mostly Irish, Scottish, English and German – were brought over as indentured servants recruited from the growing number of unemployed poor.

The Antipodes, too, were an important destination for Europeans. Since the arrival of the First Fleet in Sydney Cove on 26 January 1788 with 1,350 convicts under the command of Captain Arthur Phillip, Australia had established itself as a new destination for settlers from the British Isles. From 1815 the pace of immigration picked up as new, virtually free, lands were cultivated for farming. The discovery of gold in 1851 caused resurgent waves of European, North American and Chinese migrants. Within a ten-year period from 1850 to 1860 about 2 per cent of the population of the British Isles emigrated to New South Wales and Victoria.

In Asia there were other large movements, though less well recorded. The Chinese mass migration that continued from around 1800 to 1949 was mainly caused by war, political corruption, poverty and deprivation on the mainland. Written tallies are non-existent, and no one knows how many illiterate peasants or coolies went to countries such as the US, Australia, New Zealand, North Africa and the West Indies after the abolition of the slave trade created a shortage of manpower. It is likely to have been millions. European merchants were keen to replace African slaves with indentured labourers from China and India. A British Guiana planter found what he was looking for in the Chinese labourers – 'their strong physique, their eagerness to make money, their history of toil from infancy'.* Large numbers of unskilled Chinese were sold as labourers, in the coolie trade, in exchange for money to feed their families. Some employers promised good pay and good working conditions to get men signed on to three-year contracts. Life for a coolie was grim, and many did not live long. It was recorded on one pepper estate that out of fifty coolies hired, only two survived six months. Even if they did survive long enough to get paid, they were often cheated out of their wages and were therefore unable to afford the dreamed-of return journey home to China.

The eighteenth and nineteenth centuries are chiefly known for the Enlightenment, the birth of America, the French Revolution and its Napoleonic aftermath, the Industrial Revolution, and the rise of the British Empire. But through and around and beneath all these dramas the flow of humanity across the face of the earth accelerated. Teilhard de Chardin's vision of people moving around the sphere and completely filling it could not have been more vividly illustrated.

But that was just one part of it. Added to the mix and speeding everything along was the astonishing scientific and technical progress of the eighteenth and nineteenth centuries. Agricultural productivity in Europe, especially in Britain, increased sharply. This happened for two key reasons. First, the rising middle class who bought up farm- land in a search for secure investment were more profit-driven than landowners elsewhere in Europe, and therefore more open to new techniques. Second, agricultural science had discovered the efficiency of a four-field rotation in which the previous custom of leaving one field fallow each year was replaced by using the previously 'wasted' fallow field to grow clover and turnips. With better crop production, more livestock could be fed, leading to more protein in the diet, improved health and population growth. This new type of agriculture demanded larger tracts of land, so common land was annexed in enclosures, and many people were driven to the burgeon- ing cities to search for jobs and homes. There, the new textile mills awaited them with open gates.

If new agricultural developments freed up the labour to support

*As quoted by Lynn Pan, author of *Sons of the Yellow Emperor* (1990).

the Industrial Revolution, technological innovations were at its heart. Forced by cheap imports from India to look for a faster way to produce home-grown cloth, British textile producers developed the flying shuttle and the spinning jenny. With water-powered looms doubling the speed of textile production, mills were soon lining the riverbanks of England. And when the riverbanks filled up or water power proved insufficient, the steam engine came to the rescue, an invention whose success in turn owed much to another technological advance: the purer, stronger iron that could be produced by using large mechanized bellows to feed air into the furnaces.

Steam and textile technology; coal; a burgeoning labour force; an empire rich in raw materials; an excellent merchant-marine navy; a network of navigable inland rivers and (later) railways; and a large surplus of capital for investment: all combined to make Britain for a while the commercial hothouse of the world.

The result was a revolution that would trigger massive changes in people's living and working conditions as well as in the structures of family and society. And its energy would drive a continuous chain reaction of new technologies more or less from the eighteenth century all the way through to the present day. And these dramatic changes were not of course confined to Europe. Their power would spread across the globe, to change radically the way humanity lives.

Consider the world a hundred years ago. The first global economy had been operational for a generation. The interconnectedness of trade was firmly established. The network of supply and demand radiated from the great trading centres all around the planet. New methods of preservation meant that meat and grain from the prairies and pampas of the New World could be consumed in Europe, which paid for its imports by exporting manufactured goods. Professor J. Bradford DeLong, an economist at Berkeley, has described how the harvest west of Chicago affected grain prices in Odessa and Hamburg. The price of lambs in Auckland affected meat prices in London. Some 75 per cent of Britain's exports were manufactured goods in the years before the First World War, and textile exports made up half of Britain's manufacturing exports. By 1910, exports of goods and services amounted to more than a quarter of British,

Australian, and Canadian national product, and to perhaps a fifth of German national product.

Railways and steamships were vital in this rapidly growing trade. Until the nineteenth century, transport costs had been sufficiently high to discourage all but high-value and low-volume trade. Tariffs and other trade barriers had added another impediment. For most commodities, transport costs exceeded the price of goods in the country of origin – often substantially. Then in the nineteenth century transport costs began to fall rapidly. In addition, Britain began to cut tariffs, and many other European countries followed suit. The former deputy managing director of the International Monetary Fund, Anne Krueger, has estimated that incomes in the major producing countries doubled between 1870 and 1900, and world trade grew rapidly – at an annual rate of 3.4 per cent between 1870 and 1914.

However, with the advent of the First World War, Polanyi's 'hundred years of peace' was over. The richer industrial nations of the West plunged into a struggle from which it would take fifty years to recover. From a point where the international economy was entering the twentieth century with what Anne Krueger of the IMF has called 'the freest flow of goods, services and capital in human history', there followed the abrupt disruption of trading and financial ties. After a few faltering steps to recovery, the international economy collapsed again during the Great Depression. The rise of fascism was a direct result, followed by the horrors of the Second World War. The century-long passage towards globalization had been reversed, and would not begin any sustainable recovery until the 1950s. The story would then resume (see Chapter 4) with new and even greater impetus, as if the genie of international enterprise had been bottled for almost half a century with the pressure slowly building all the time.

First, though, we need to look at the role of money and capital in all this.

From the first, capital was intrinsic to commerce and an essential lubricant of trade. Even in prehistoric times, before the development of common measures of value or media of exchange, credit probably existed. Anthropological evidence suggests that the earliest prehistoric loans were of seeds or of animals. Both were loans for productive purposes. Seeds yielded an increase. Animals reproduced. Both could eventually be returned with interest. The notion of animals as a measure of wealth is rooted in the etymology of the modern language of finance – as evidenced by the common origins of words such as 'capital', 'chattels' and 'cattle' and the source of the word 'pecuniary' (from the Latin *pecus,* meaning 'flock'). Early Greeks measured precious metals in cattle; one of Penelope's suitors in the *Odyssey* promises to bring Odysseus 'bronze and gold to the value of twenty oxen'.

By the earliest historical times, loans with interest had become common. We know this because they were eventually codified around 1800 BC by Hammurabi, one of the kings of ancient Babylonia. One of the earliest known sets of credit rules, the codes state that all loans had to be recorded in writing before appointed officials, and that for a loan of grain the maximum rate of interest was 33.3 per cent per annum, payable in kind. Effectively, as cattle and grain became available in quantities above consumption requirements, these provided a form of primitive currency. They became commodities of sufficient value and uniformity that they could be used as a standard medium of exchange for other commodities. At one time or another, amber, beads, cowry shells, drums, eggs, feathers, gongs, hoes, ivory, jade, kettles, leather, mats, nails, oxen, pigs, quartz, rice, salt, thimbles and zappozaps (decorated axes) have all been used as currency. Well into the twentieth century the Kirghiz of the Russian steppes used horses as their main monetary unit. (Small change was given in lambskins.) Cigarettes were used in this way in prisoner-of-war camps in the Second World War.

Yet there was a more efficient system: money. For most of its history, money existed alongside commodity exchange – at first as an advanced system for a minority of the world's more sophisticated traders (the earliest known coins, found at the Temple of Artemis at Ephesus, date back to 600 BC) and, from the seventeenth century (with the universal recognition of 'pieces of eight', silver Spanish dollars worth eight reales), as something akin to the global pattern of notes and coins that we know today. In his 2008 book *The*

Ascent of Money: A Financial History of the World, the historian Niall Ferguson summarizes the six characteristics that healthily functioning money must have: availability, affordability, durability, fungibility (i.e. interchangeability), portability and reliability. For thousands of years gold, silver and bronze fitted the purpose, and by Roman times were ranked in that order according to the relative scarcity of the metals – an order that is now synonymous everywhere in the sporting world with first, second and third places.

The story of money is of a development from commodities to coinage to representative money and finally, in the twentieth century, to fiat money (where the value lies solely in the promise rather than in reserves of another commodity such as gold). The tipping point in the story was the growth of representative money. To transfer the sense of value from a usable material object to an abstract symbol of value was a major social and psychological step. Representative money includes the warehouse receipts issued by the ancient Egyptian grain banks, paper currency in seventh-century China, the receipts issued by England's goldsmith bankers, bills of exchange based on tradable goods, and more recent forms of paper or metal currency that were backed by gold or silver.

Money made buying and selling far more efficient. Without money, barter between different staples created multiple different possible exchange pairs and prices. With money there are only as many prices as goods. Money eliminated inefficiencies by providing a unit of account (enabling easier valuations) and a store of value (allowing transactions over long distances and varied time periods). It facilitated accurate bookkeeping. And it gave banking the basis for explosive growth.

Rudimentary banking practices had been in existence since the beginning. Loans, deposits and exchange were taking place well before the invention of money. As early as the third millennium BC, these functions were performed by temples. Deposits would have been initially grain, then other goods such as cattle, and then gold. Transfers of wealth became simpler, and a deposit in one place could be paired with a withdrawal in another. For example, when Egypt fell under the rule of the Greeks in the fourth century BC, government granaries were transformed into a network of grain banks centralized in Alexandria, where the main accounts were recorded. Less than a century later, the Aegean island of Delos became a prominent banking centre, where cash transactions were replaced by credit receipts, and accounts were kept for each client. Subsequently the Romans refined the administration of banking and saw greater regulation of financial practices, including charging interest on loans and paying interest on deposits. The fall of Rome and the advent of the Dark Ages interrupted the process. Banking was largely abandoned in Europe, as civilization collapsed and connections withered.

Banking revived in Italian towns during the Middle Ages. Ferguson shows how the famous Medici family of Florence made the transition from financial success to hereditary status and power. Their four-teenth-century *libro segreto* or 'secret book' is a meticulous record of reserves and deposits on one side and loans and commercial bills on the other. The core of the business was bills of exchange. These enabled trade creditors to get immediate cash (at a discount) in exchange for allowing bankers to recover what was due to them. In the discount lay the source of the bankers' profit. By the time Cosimo de' Medici took over the business, in 1420, there were branches of the family bank in Venice and Rome, to which he added Geneva, Pisa, London and Avignon. And it was this Italian system that became the model for the most successful northern European nations: the Dutch, the Swedes and the British. Each made a key contribution to the banking story. The Amsterdam Exchange Bank, set up in 1609, pioneered direct transfers that allowed transactions to take place without the need for physical money. In 1656 the Swedish Riksbank invented fractional reserve banking, i.e. creating credit by lending more than its cash reserves. And in 1742 the Bank of England established a partial monopoly on the issue of banknotes (a promissory note without interest), which allowed transactions without the need for the parties involved to have current accounts. The development of money and banking had made lending and investment possible in multiple new ways.

And the world became a better place. At a time when public trust

in the financial markets is at a very low ebb, we need to remind ourselves of the basic truth that, as Ferguson puts it, 'A world without
money would be worse, much worse, than our present world. It is
wrong to think (as Shakespeare's Antonio did) of all lenders of
money as mere leeches, sucking the life's blood out of unfortunate
debtors ... Credit and debt, in short, are among the essential building blocks of economic development, as vital to creating the wealth
of nations as mining, manufacturing or mobile telephony.'

But the role of money and capital has always been controversial:
some have more than others; debts and interest have to be repaid,
borrowing can be a last resort. This led to a range of moral strictures
from religious and philosophical leaders that profoundly influenced
the shape of banking.

Early Judaeo-Christian biblical teaching was hostile to lending
money for interest. Augustine, writing in the fifth century, called
such 'usury' a crime. Led by the indefatigable Pope Alexander III,
the Third Lateran Council in 1179 re-established the point: 'Nearly
everywhere the crime of usury has become so firmly rooted that
many, omitting other business, practise usury as if it were permitted,
and in no way observe how it is forbidden in both the Old and New
Testament. We therefore declare that notorious usurers should not
be admitted to communion of the altar or receive Christian burial if
they die in this sin.'

In 1311 the Church's positioned hardened still further, when Pope
Clement V made the ban on usury absolute, and declared all secular
legislation in its favour to be null and void and any defence of usury
to be heresy. In the spirit of the times, Dante in *The Divine Comedy*
has usurers confined to an inner ring of the seventh circle of hell – a
desert of flaming sand.

For Jews, too, usury was forbidden – although only within the
community: 'You may charge interest to a foreigner, but to your
countrymen you shall not charge interest, so that the Lord your God
may bless you in all that you undertake in the land which you are
about to enter to possess' (Deuteronomy 23:20–21).

This meant that a Jew might lend to anyone who was not a Jew.
As James Carroll points out in his 2001 book *Constantine's Sword*:

The Church and the Jews, this was not the only reason that the Jews came to be characterized as the moneylenders of Europe, but it was instrumental. Other factors were that Jews had been forbidden to own land and so were more mobile than Christians. Thus encouraged to be peripatetic, they became useful carriers of money and therefore a ready source of currency exchange. It helped too that, marginalized by religious custom, they were able to keep a useful professional distance from their customers. The most famous moneylender of all, Shylock, in *The Merchant of Venice*, makes the point: 'I will buy with you, sell with you, talk with you, walk with you, and so following, but I will not eat with you, drink with you, nor pray with you.'

Jews were not the only moneylenders in medieval society. In other parts of the world it was the Christians who took on this role. The Armenians, for instance, one of the oldest Christian communities in the world, became the bankers to the (Muslim) Turks. Later, the expansion of the Ottoman Empire was extensively financed by a network of Armenian bankers. But moneylenders are rarely popular in any society. When the moneylenders are cultural outsiders, paranoia and resentment can give rise to terrible atrocities in times of social stress. In the case of European Jewry, above all, the combination of resentment and religious prejudice boiled over regularly into horrific pogroms, from which virtually no country has been immune, and which culminated in the Holocaust, the stain of which will be on the conscience of Europe for the rest of history.

Not only was biblical teaching hostile to moneylending for interest, so was that other pervasive influence on European thought, Aristotle. Though he lived and worked in the fourth century BC, Aristotle's writings dominated intellectual life for centuries. From ancient times through to the Renaissance, his influence spread. His works were translated into Latin, Syriac, Arabic, Italian, French, German and English. His thinking was a major influence on Islamic philosophy: Averroës, that most famous of all Arab philosophers, attempted to create a synthesis of Islamic theology and Aristotelian rationalism. Maimonides, among the most influential of medieval Jewish thinkers, created a similar synthesis for Judaism. In the

Christian thought-world, the most celebrated Aristotelian synthesis was the *Summa Theologica* of the thirteenth century scholar Thomas Aquinas. On the subject of usury, all of them broadly followed the line of their master: 'The most hated sort [of wealth getting] and with the greatest reason, is usury, which makes a gain out of money itself and not from the natural object of it. For money was intended to be used in exchange but not to increase at interest' (Aristotle, *Politics*, I).

Aristotle declared that lending money for interest was wholly unnatural and devoid of virtue. Money was barren: it didn't itself create anything, and therefore had no right to be rewarded for anything. Aristotelian disapproval is ubiquitous in early theological discussions of commercial ethics: in fact Aristotelian elements are often detectable in Christian commentary on finance to this day. At the height of medieval Christian influence over Europe, the attitude to commerce and finance was formed on the basis of a Jewish heritage which considered it exploitative and buttressed by a Greek world view which held it to be unnatural. No wonder that the result was so unmistakably hostile.

Islam too was unequivocal. The criticism of usury in Islam was well established during the Prophet Muhammad's life. The original word used for usury in the *Koran* was *riba*, which literally means 'excess'.

Those who charge usury are in the same position as those controlled by the Devil's influence. This is because they claim that usury is the same as commerce. However, God permits commerce, and prohibits usury. Thus, whoever heeds this commandment from his Lord, and refrains from usury, he may keep his past earnings, and his judgement rests with God. As for those who persist in usury, they incur hell, wherein they abide for ever.

(The *Koran*, al-Baqarah 2:275)

By the end of the seventh century the prohibition of interest was a well-established working principle integrated into the Islamic economic system. While far from universally practised in the Islamic world, sharia-compliant finance has in recent years seen a major resurgence in Muslim commerce, where the emphasis is on investment, with the risk shared by the investor as well as the entrepreneur, rather than lending at interest, which remains unacceptable.

In China too, money and trade were treated with suspicion by bureaucrats and landowners. The prevailing Confucian ethos was markedly hostile to the whole process of profit-making commerce, which it saw as intrinsically threatening and untrustworthy. As stated in the *Analects* of Confucius, rather haughtily, 'The gentleman is familiar with what is right, just as the small man is familiar with profit.' The resistance to what Confucius's followers instinctively knew was a revolutionary force clearly echoes the dislike of money-lenders in Europe. In both cases, the hostility drew on upper-class concerns about the destabilizing impact of commerce and on the resentment of the poor, who often ended up in hopeless debt.

In Europe, though, there was no single force powerful enough to keep commerce in check. So the tension between ideology and practice became more and more acute. From the fifteenth century onward, as trade began to flourish, the demand for loans broadened. Somewhat uncomfortably, theologians began to accommodate commerce by finding ways to allow finance which did not count as usury. But it would take a revolutionary theologian in tune with the new urban trading classes to make the decisive break and define an acceptable role for lending money with interest.

John Calvin was lucid, cold, courageous, one of the great prose stylists of French literature, and the de-facto ruler of Geneva, one of Europe's main financial hubs, in the mid sixteenth century. Calvin dealt simply with the old orthodoxy about the evils of finance. He stated bluntly that the Old Testament was no longer relevant, because a new Christian era had replaced the ancient society of the Israelites. The new law was a law of love. There could be no objection to loans at reasonable interest rates between parties who had good business reasons to lend and to borrow. He wrote, 'Usury is not now unlawful, except insofar as it contravenes equity and brotherly union.' The shift was radical – although it stopped a long way short of being a gospel for a free market. It was accompanied by an equally radical shift in the idea of vocation. Before the Reformation, the notion of a vocation had been reserved for clerical positions. Luther made space for the idea that there could be vocations to secular roles, but limited them to simple agricultural and craft activities. Calvin went much further, arguing that if you had money you were a steward of God and must use what you had been entrusted with. This meant that investment and banking could be spiritually legitimate activities. Moneylenders could come in from the cold.

The next great leap was that of the great eighteenth-century Scottish economist Adam Smith. If Calvin had allowed moneylenders a place in the kingdom of heaven, Smith opened the way to placing the world of commerce and finance on the same morally impregnable level as the world of nature. It was Smith's work that allowed his contemporary Edmund Burke to state, 'The laws of commerce are the laws of nature, and therefore the laws of God.'

What had Smith done? He was the first economist fully to understand the importance of competition. Its existence had been recognized, of course, but it had been condemned as nothing but combative greed and totally inconsistent with the spirit of Christian life. Smith put the role of competition at the centre of economic progress. His famous metaphor of 'the invisible hand', introduced in 1759 in *The Theory of Moral Sentiments*, has come to stand for the idea that if each consumer is allowed to choose freely what to buy and each producer is allowed to choose freely what to sell and how to produce it, the market will settle on a pattern of distribution and price that is beneficial to all the individual members of a community, and hence to the community as a whole. Self-interest will lead to collectively beneficial behaviour. The search for maximum profits will drive the adoption of efficient methods of production. The pressure to undercut competition will drive prices down. Industries that are necessary and useful will have better returns, and so, naturally, investors will be attracted to them and away from businesses that are marginal or inefficient, which deliver less attractive returns. Students will prepare for the most remunerative – and by implication the most necessary – careers. And this process will be self-generating. It will happen automatically. The invisible hand seemed to leave no room for the issue of commercial right and wrong even to get on to the agenda. Theology appeared to have lost its time-honoured role as arbiter of commercial morality. (It was not clear what would replace it. As we shall see, this is an issue that is still with us to the this day.)

If Adam Smith had laid the foundations for the first basic principle of globalization – the importance of free markets based on free competition – the other was laid by the political economist David Ricardo. Inspired by reading Smith's *The Wealth of Nations* (1776) while on holiday in Bath, Ricardo published his most famous work, *Principles of Political Economy and Taxation*, in 1817. In it he developed the 'law of comparative advantage', which became the classic account of the benefit of trade to both parties involved. He showed that there was benefit in two countries trading in two goods even if one of the countries produced *both* goods more efficiently than the other, as long as each country concentrated on the product it was *relatively* more efficient at making. The example he used was the nineteenth-century wine and cloth trade between England and Portugal. In Portugal it was possible to produce both wine and cloth for a lower absolute cost than it would take to produce the same quantities in England. However, it was relatively far more efficient for England to produce cloth than wine (unsurprisingly, given the climate). Therefore, while it was cheaper to produce cloth in Portugal than in England, it was more beneficial for Portugal to produce wine for export and trade that for English cloth. Conclusion: each country gains by specializing in the good in which it has *comparative* advantage. Ricardo's argument remains to this day the underlying theoretical basis for the free flow of goods between nations.

Over a period of fewer than sixty years, the ideas of competition and free trade had found their definitive intellectual champions. Between them, Smith and Ricardo set the theoretical course of the globalized industrial and commercial world. But the sailing wasn't always going to be plain.

The resistance was sustained and powerful, spanning philosophy, social science and literature. The roots had already been laid by

Romantic opposition to industrialization – Goethe's *Naturphilo-sophie*, William Blake's 'dark, satanic mills', and William Words-worth's attack in *Lyrical Ballads* on the 'savage torpor' of the mechanized mind, and much more. As the nineteenth century progressed, the anti-commercial torch was carried by other literary figures such as Elizabeth Gaskell, the Brontë sisters, Elizabeth Barrett Browning, William Thackeray, and above all the two greatest novelists of the industrial age: Charles Dickens in England and Emile Zola in France. Here is Dickens' description of the fictional industrial netherworld Coketown, from *Hard Times* (1854):

It was a town of machinery and tall chimneys, out of which interminable serpents of smoke trailed themselves for ever and ever, and never got uncoiled. It had a black canal in it, and a river that ran purple with ill-smelling dye, and vast piles of building full of windows where there was a rattling and a trembling all day long, and where the piston of the steam-engine worked monotonously up and down, like the head of an elephant in a state of melancholy madness.

Thirty years later the mechanized monotony portrayed by Dickens has become actively cannibalistic in the hands of Zola. Here, in *Germinal* (1885), he describes the fictional mine Le Voreux ('the Voracious One'):

The tall blast furnaces and the coke ovens blazed, turning the darkness blood-red without illuminating the unknown. And the Voreux, at the bottom of its hole, crouching like an evil beast, continued to crunch, breathing heavily and slowly as if troubled by its painful digestion of human flesh.

It was not only novelists who viewed the outworkings of the Industrial Revolution with outrage. Friedrich Engels (whose talent as a reporter is under-appreciated) explored Manchester during a spell working for the family firm:

The view ... is characteristic for the whole district. At the bottom flows, or rather stagnates, the Irk, a narrow, coal-black, foul-smelling stream, full of debris and refuse, which it deposits on the shallower right bank. In dry weather, a long string of the most disgusting, blackish-green, slime pools are left standing on this bank, from the depths of which bubbles of miasmatic gas constantly arise and give forth a stench unendurable even on the bridge forty or fifty feet above the surface of the stream. But besides this, the stream itself is checked every few paces by high weirs, behind which slime and refuse accumulate and rot in thick masses ... Below the bridge you look upon the piles of debris, the refuse, filth, and offal from the courts on the steep left bank; here each house is packed close behind its neighbour and a piece of each is visible, all black, smoky, crumbling, ancient, with broken panes and window frames

(The Condition of the Working-Class in England in 1844)

Karl Marx, whose ideological opposition to the philosophy of the market became one of the defining intellectual monuments of the century, was more scientific but just as passionate and as powerful in his writing. No student of the horror of the Victorian industrial system should omit Chapter 10 of Volume 1 of *Das Kapital* (1867) – an unsparingly meticulous record of factory conditions taken in 1863. Marx quotes a report in – of all places – the *Daily Telegraph* which recorded that:

There was an amount of privation and suffering among that portion of the population connected with the lace trade, unknown in other parts of the kingdom, indeed, in the civilized world ... Children of nine or ten years are dragged from their squalid beds at two, three or four o'clock in the morning and compelled to work for a bare subsistence until ten, eleven or twelve at night, their limbs wearing away, their frames dwindling, their faces whitening and their humanity absolutely sinking into a stone-like torpor`... We declaim against the Virginian and Carolinian cotton-planters. Is their black-market, their lash and their barter of human flesh more detestable than this slow sacrifice of humanity which takes place in order that veils and collars may be fabricated for the benefit of capitalists?

The heartlessness of reason, the tyranny of mechanization, the greed of industrialists and the exploitation of innocence were arguments powerfully made and songs powerfully sung. And by the start of the twentieth century they had come together and developed into an overarching theoretical preoccupation for the developed world: was capitalism the answer or the problem?

For some, such as John Stuart Mill, the private ownership of capital was an essential underpinning of human freedom. Published in 1848, Mill's *Principles of Political Economy* was the dominant economics textbook in the English language through to the end of the nineteenth century. At the heart of his thinking was a defence of the benefits of free competition and the encouragement of individual initiative and responsibility. Although he recognized that the benefits of individualism did not free the state from its responsibility to provide security for its citizens, Mill modified his generally laissez-faire stance to only a limited extent, to argue that private monopolies must be prevented, the poor must be properly looked after, and education must be provided for children.

For others, such as the French anarchist philosopher Pierre-Joseph Proudhon, born within three years of Mill and writing over the same period, capitalism was intrinsically exploitative. In *What is Property?* (1840) Proudhon famously declared that 'property is theft', and argued against many of the property rights prevalent in nineteenth-century France – especially all those rights of property which conferred effective control of another human being. He saw capitalism as part of the machinery of tyranny: 'What capital does to labour, and the state to liberty, the Church does to the spirit. This trinity of absolutism is as baneful in practice as it is in philosophy. The most effective means for oppressing the people would be simultaneously to enslave its body, its will and its reason' (*The Confessions of a Revolutionary* (1851)).

For Proudhon's one-time friend Karl Marx and his disciples, capitalism was intrinsically unstable and contained the seeds of its own self-destruction. More and more capital would become concentrated in fewer and fewer hands; more and more workers would be paid less and less. Competition (including the competition made possible by trade) would drive down wages, prices and profitability. Marx argued that at a certain point the economic structure of capitalism would no longer be able to contain the ever-developing productive forces of society. There would be a crisis of capitalism resolved only by revolution by the working class – the one element in society that had no stake in the system. Marx was part historical determinist, part Romantic who was revolted by the alienation and suffering he documented, and part Promethean optimist who saw the proletariat defiantly seizing and realizing its own utopian future. As the revolution unfolded, power would flow to the proletariat, and a communist and classless economy would follow.

Looking back a century and a half later, we have seen the mutation of this vision into the brutality of Stalinism during the twentieth century. As a species, we are older and wiser. But viewing it against the background of the nineteenth-century Industrial Revolution, it is easy to understand the appeal of Marx as the twentieth century dawned.

And then there was another view, less well known but potentially more durable, which saw money and the process of exchange itself as changing humanity by individualizing and alienating people. The principal exponent of this thesis, Georg Simmel, was born in Berlin in 1858 and was in many respects one of the founders of modern sociology. Unlike Marx, he focused on the effect of commerce and urbanization not so much on class structures as on the consciousness of the individual. In *The Philosophy of Money* (1900) he discusses the sense in which money 'intervenes between person and person' by objectifying and fragmenting social relations, in the same way as it 'intervenes between person and commodity' by distancing individual activity from its ultimate meaning and purpose. He is not, however, arguing for a rejection of money and commerce. He is observing that the nature of modern, urbanized humanity is vitally determined by the fact of the money economy. In this he is a forerunner of Polanyi. He accepts that we are intrinsically commercial beings and that commerce individualizes us in certain inevitable ways – a theme we shall return to later. It is a view which is much more consistent with the essence of the globalized and urbanized twenty-first century than is the class-based thought-world of Marx.

Perhaps as important as the theoretical debate was the practical debate about the relative strengths of the state and the private sector in efficiently deploying capital for development. This ideological battle-ground was fought over throughout much of the twentieth century.

At the free-market end of the spectrum there has always been one dominant ideological representative, the US. The US is the one major country that might be said to have the ideology of free-market capitalism in its genes. 'America is the Canaan of capitalism, its promised land,' the German economist Werner Sombart wrote in 1906. From the first, US railroad magnates and industrial barons had enormous scope for expansion with relatively little state or social restraint. In fact, however, what is striking about a country where the word 'socialism' has always been a term of abuse or derision is the extent to which government has intervened pragmatically at times of crisis (in the 1930s and in 2008/9, for example) and has found itself involved, directly or implicitly, more deeply and for far longer than it intended – as evidenced in, for example, the saga of the mortgage institutions Freddie Mac and Fannie Mae. Nevertheless, Calvin Coolidge was right: 'The business of America is business.' There is no other major country in the world of which this would sound so much like a truism.

At the other end of the spectrum have been the huge and radical social-engineering projects undertaken in the twentieth century – in the Soviet Union of the 1930s and in the China of the Great Leap Forward of 1958–61. For a while, both countries were perhaps able to convince themselves (and others) of their ability to achieve faster growth, greater fairness and more staying power than under a liberal market approach. In particular, the Soviet Union managed to remain relatively immune to the effects of the Great Depression. But only at horrendous human cost. And eventually, by the 1980s, it was becoming clear that the vaunted economic achievements were all too hollow and that the ability to compete with a newly vibrant post-war international economy led by the US was declining fast.

For a while, much of the rest of the world followed a path which could be considered a kind of 'third way' – or rather found itself somewhere in the middle of the spectrum. India, for example, was for most of the period since independence a highly planned, socialist-inspired – yet democratic – economy. Typically, too, European societies (including Britain) have had a central tendency influenced by a pervasive belief in the responsibility of government actively to intervene for the social good. It would be wrong, of course, to overlook important differences among the Europeans: in particular, the Enlightenment in Britain took a more individualist, less *étatiste*, form than in France. This difference between the two countries consistently manifests itself in their social and political thinking to this day. Conversely, it is always possible to overstate the differences between Europe and the US: since the 1980s, the enthusiasm for the sort of indicative industrial planning which was prevalent in Europe in the earlier post-war decades has waned significantly. Nonetheless, the centre of gravity of European economic and social politics has clearly been different from that of the US.

By the end of the twentieth century, however, even the practical debate had run out of steam. By the millennium, there were few left who were prepared to ignore the mounting evidence of inflexibility, inefficiency and corruption which result from the state playing a major role in capital investment. Emblematic images come to mind. Deng Xiaoping, who once remarked, 'I don't care if the cat is black or white, so long as it catches mice,' looking across the Chinese border at thriving, capitalist Hong Kong in 1979 and giving his blessing to China's burgeoning private sector; the crowds swarming over the Berlin Wall on 9 November 1989; jubilation in front of Romanian television screens at the time of the downfall and execution of the communist dictator Nicolae Ceauşescu and his wife in December 1989; the first McDonald's opening in Moscow, on 31 January 1990; the decree banning the Russian Communist Party, on 6 November 1991. A new consensus was emerging: it even had a name – the Washington Consensus (after the package of open-market-oriented policy prescriptions promoted for developing countries by the International Monetary Fund, the World Bank and the US Treasury Department). In the early 1990s, India began significant liberalization. In various ways, with varying degrees of radicalism, other emerging markets did the same. Liberal capitalism seemed to be in the ascendant everywhere.

*

Was the collapse of communism the triumph of another ism? No. Capitalism is not just another ism in the sense of communism, socialism, or fascism. It is not just a system imposed on societies or chosen by them: more fundamentally, the propensity to venture and trade is the default mode of human economic interaction. In the young and expanding field of evolutionary psychology, features of human nature are being traced back to their roots in our ancestors' struggle for survival fifty thousand years ago. Some of them – that humanity tends to be hierarchical – might not seem to be obviously consistent with capitalism. But other traits point another way. That property rights are natural and even prefigured in nature by the way many animals mark out territories for foraging, hunting and mating is one clear example. Most significantly, trade and mutually beneficial exchange seem to be human universals, as is the division of labour. The American psychologist Leda Cosmides and her anthropologist husband John Tooby have shown that hunter-gatherers were involved in numerous forms of trade and exchange, and that some forms of hunter-gatherer trading can involve quite complex specialization and the interaction of supply and demand. In other words, the human mind seems to have evolved in a way that is 'built' to trade. Capitalism emerges when other isms aren't imposed. It can be suppressed, but it always reappears. In this sense it is the precise parallel of what was said about globalization in Chapter 2.

To acknowledge this is not to be naive about capitalism. Historians, industrialists and politicians have often gone on to argue that allowing capitalism its head would be the most powerful way of achieving material progress and liberal democracy that the world has ever known. In a *Financial Times* column of January 2008 Gideon Rachman cited some of the leading optimists. There was the famous essay 'The End of History?', published in 1989 in the Washington magazine the *National Interest*, in which Francis Fukuyama suggested that liberal democracy – with its inevitably capitalistic economic form – 'may constitute the end point of man's ideological evolution'. In 1993 Rupert Murdoch contended that advances in communications technology had 'proved an unambiguous threat to totalitarian regimes'. In 2000 Bill Clinton suggested that liberty would be spread inexorably 'by cell phone and cable modem'. Yet twenty years after the 'end of history' the world financial system has been convulsed, and it is not at all obvious that the confident predictions of the liberal, democratic determinists will be realized. Adam Smith would be unsurprised. Though the intellectual father of capitalism, he was never so credulous. It is sometimes overlooked that throughout his life he expressed grave reservations about un-trammelled capitalism, especially the threat it poses to the public interest. For example, in *The Wealth of Nations* he noted caustically that:

The proposal of any new law or regulation which comes from [businessmen] ought always to be listened to with great precaution, and ought never to be adopted till after having been long and carefully examined, not only with the most scrupulous but with the most suspicious attention. It comes from an order of men whose interest is never exactly the same with that of the public, who have generally an interest to deceive and even to oppress the public, and who accordingly have upon many occasions both deceived and oppressed it.

Smith knew that, in following its capitalist instincts, humanity would be riding a tiger.

The grand sweep of the story, however, has an overwhelming shape and meaning. From trading obsidian flakes to opening branches of McDonald's in Moscow and Beijing, despite continuing resistance expressed in religion, philosophy and literature, human-ity's aptitude for commerce has been unstoppable. At the heart of it has been the instinct to explore and connect. Survival gave humanity legs; trade lent it wings. Within two thousand years the world went from isolated pockets of civilization sending out traders like messengers to other worlds, to a seething mass of ceaseless exchanges of money, goods and ideas in which no individual in any corner of the world could be untouched. John Donne's famous phrase 'No man is an island' spoke of the human condition in all its complexity – the complexity of the individual as part of the human tapestry, separate and yet part of the whole. Teilhard de Chardin's vision was that only by oneness with the whole is there in fact any meaning or basis for the one. Yet at the heart of this human condition is a capitalist commercial instinct which is profoundly ambiguous in its impact on human relationships.

Does all this mean that humanity is now on the home stretch to a new Jerusalem? That is the question for the next chapter.

4

The Home Stretch to a
New Jerusalem?

Where is the Life we have lost in living?
Where is the wisdom we have lost in knowledge?
Where is the knowledge we have lost in information?
T. S. Eliot, Choruses from *The Rock* (1934)

The defining moment of the world in the twentieth century is 1914. There are other major watersheds, of course: the Russian Revolution, Hiroshima, the establishment of the People's Republic of China, the events of 1989 – or the day that Tim Berners-Lee launched the notion of the World Wide Web. But August 1914 remains the century's biggest rupture between what came before and what came after – a huge shock to the belief that had steadily grown from the end of the eighteenth century in Europe to the start of the twentieth, that progress was inevitable. 'The lamps are going out all over Europe; we shall not see them lit again in our lifetime', famously intoned British Foreign Secretary Sir Edward Grey on 4 August 1914. He was essentially right. The First World War may have ended in 1918; but the lights of progress, global integration and economic expansion remained out until at least the 1950s – two generations later. And the earthquake of August 1914, with its consequences for international relationships, the decay of stable political structures and the rise of political extremism, was not just of European significance, but global.

It is sometimes said that the First World War did not end until 1945, or even until 1989. When the war officially ended, in 1918, the results set the stage for the next twenty years. The Germans deeply resented the Treaty of Versailles. Much of the map of Europe was redrawn by the victors in line with the theory that future wars could be prevented if ethnic groups had their own homeland; yet this created instability from the Baltic to the Balkans. The Russian Revolution of 1917 had sent shock waves through the world, and was then hijacked by a Stalin interested not in 'socialist world revolution', but in the forced industrialization and collectivization of the Soviet state. Meanwhile, festering German resentments and national shame helped to propel the rise of Hitler and his new variant of fascism – Nazism – which found easy recruits for its theories of racial purity and supremacy in the widespread contemporary European anti-Semitism and xenophobia fuelled by the Great Depression. Western ambivalence towards Nazi expansionism was given some oxygen by a desire to see a strong Germany settling the balance with Stalin's Russia. Japan too was misunderstood – both its emerging power and its regional ambitions. The mistakes and hesitations culminated in the Second World War. And in the aftermath of that came the state of acrid tension that effectively held the balance of global power from the mid-1940s to 1989: the Cold War between the United States and the Soviet Union.

Economically, the First World War left the world scarred in a way that it would never, to this day, entirely forget. The hyperinflation that followed in Germany was not the first case in the world, nor the only example of hyperinflation in Europe at the time (Austria and the Soviet Union also suffered), but it was by far the most prominent case up to that point – and the most serious ever to have occurred in a major industrialized economy. The extraordinary consequences associated with hyperinflation were first systematically documented in Germany: repeated redenomination of the currency; the flight from cash; exponential increases in prices and interest rates. In 1922 the highest-denomination banknote in Germany was 50,000 marks; by 1923 it was 100 billion marks. The devastating experience burned itself into the folk memory of the German people, and even now, at several removes, it still arguably influences how Germans think and behave. The power of folk memories from the early decades of the twentieth century continues to stalk the world in other ways too: what the Somme is to Britain and hyperinflation is to Germany, so the Great Depression is to contemporary America.

But from 1950, though there was no sudden 'glad confident morning' for the world, signs emerged that the clouds were beginning to clear. One patch of blue sky was tariff reform. The first half of the twentieth century had seen the world throw up trade barriers with growing enthusiasm. America led in its isolationism and protectionism, and learned – the hard way – that isolation is not an option in the modern world, and that protectionism invites retaliation. As the US emerged from the horrors of the Second World War, it began the task of taking down the barriers erected over most of the preceding century. William J. Bernstein has unearthed a State Department report published in 1945 – *Proposals for the Expansion of Trade and Employment* – that, as he says, effectively sets out the road map for today's globalized economy. The key task that the authors identified was to negotiate the unravelling of the protectionism that had increasingly crippled international commerce since 1880. In early 1947, trade officials from twenty-two nations met in Geneva using the State Department proposals as their starting point. On 17 November 1947 the General Agreement on Tariffs and Trade (GATT) was signed by all participants. GATT, perhaps against the odds, flourished through many rounds of successive talks culminating in the Uruguay Round in 1986, after which the process was handed to the World Trade Organization. The average applied tariff level of the US, UK, France and Germany had risen from around 15 per cent in 1913 to around 30 per cent in 1932; since 1945 it has fallen significantly, and now sits at something less than 5 per cent. The effect of this on trade has been dramatic. If the nineteenth century saw trade expand owing to reduced transport costs, in the twentieth it was owing chiefly to plummeting tariffs.

If tariff reform unblocked the flow of world trade, then the liberalization of capital markets that followed it unblocked the flow of money. One of the opening acts of Margaret Thatcher's new government in 1979 was the abolition of UK exchange controls. Seven years later came 'Big Bang', a root-and-branch reform of the

London capital markets. The effects were dramatic. London's place as a financial capital was decisively strengthened; this was the beginning of its role as the great intellectual crossroads of a globalizing world economy (of which more later). Ronald Reagan's administration followed Thatcher's lead. Country after country loosened up its regulations, not necessarily completely; but the effect was a significant increase in the freedom of capital flows across borders throughout much of the world.

Then the last decade of the century saw radical change sweep through what became known – rather significantly – as the emerging markets. And no change was more radical or more important than the return of China to full participation in the global bazaar. Deng Xiaoping was confirmed as paramount leader in December 1978. His new, pragmatic, leadership emphasized economic development and renounced mass political movements. Immediately he launched the 'Four Modernizations': the modernization of agriculture, industry, and science and technology, as well as the military. The aim was clear: to turn China into an uncompromisingly modern industrial nation. And the strategy had a description: 'socialism with Chinese characteristics'. It opened a new era in Chinese history.

Deng emphasized that socialism did not mean shared poverty, and policies should not be rejected on the grounds that they were similar to those found in capitalist nations. He allowed management of the macroeconomy through market mechanisms, and much of it was modelled on economic planning and control mechanisms in Western nations. At the local level, material incentives rather than political appeals were to be used to motivate the labour force, beginning with allowing peasants to earn extra income by selling the produce of their private plots on the free market. Local municipalities and provinces were free to invest in the industries that they considered most profitable, which encouraged investment in light manufacturing. Thus Deng's reforms shifted China's development strategy to emphasize light industry and export-led growth. Not for nothing has this period been described as China's Industrial Revolution.

Then India too, the largest democracy in the world, also began to open up, bringing hundreds of millions of people into the bazaar. By the early 1990s the Indian economy was on the brink of collapse. After a generation of bureaucratic state-planned development, the government was close to default, and foreign-exchange reserves had shrunk to the point that India could barely finance three weeks' worth of imports. The government headed by Narasimha Rao launched reforms designed by finance minister Manmohan Singh, who later became prime minister, aimed at opening up the country to foreign investment, reforming capital markets, deregulating domestic business, and liberalizing the trade regime. The impact of these reforms was clear. Total foreign investment in India began to rise, and economic growth accelerated. Foreign-exchange reserves rose from under $5 billion to over $100 billion within ten years.

The changes in China and India, together with the opening-up of eastern Europe and the demise of the Soviet Union, meant that some 3 billion people joined an increasingly connected global market. And, in the end, the striking characteristic of economic activity in the second half of the twentieth century is its staggering size and acceleration when compared with developments in previous centuries. The total amount of goods and services produced in that period may well have matched the cumulative total output over the whole of recorded human history up to then.

The twentieth century also saw an explosion of the world population – from 1.6 billion people at the beginning of the century to around 6.5 billion at the end. The last three decades have, moreover, seen a surge in migration again. The foreign-born population of the US, for example, is now at an all-time high, at nearly 40 million. There are now nineteen cities in the world with foreign-born populations of over 1 million (including London, Paris and nine US cities).

Simultaneously, the distribution of the world's wealth has become more unequal. The richest quarter of the world population has seen its per-capita GDP increase close to sixfold over the century, while per-capita income for the poorest quarter has increased less than threefold. From a long-term historical perspective, this still represents a notable acceleration of income growth. Nevertheless, the levels of GDP per person toward the end of the century in many poor countries were in real terms still well below those already attained by the leading countries in 1900. The level of GDP per person in Africa in 1900 was about one-ninth of that of the leading countries at the time. But by 2000 the ratio was even lower, at about one-twentieth. Economic growth in the poorest countries over the 1990s was insufficient to reduce the absolute number in extreme poverty, which remains to this day at over 1 billion.

Nevertheless, recent studies have shown that over about the last thirty years the majority of the world's poor have for the first time achieved income growth faster than in developed countries. Many populous economies, including Pakistan, Bangladesh and Indonesia, have experienced strong real per-capita GDP growth over the last two decades, notwithstanding the Asian crisis of the late 1990s. But it is China and India that have really made the difference. Together they account for almost 40 per cent of the world's population, and both were formerly extremely poor. Their rapid recent economic progress, consequent on their policy reforms of the last two decades, has had a clear impact on development statistics.

The experience of transformation in China and India in the last twenty years has received increasingly rapt attention and analysis because of their sheer size. Both nations wield increasing diplomatic clout in the international corridors of power. Their emergence on the world stage is profoundly changing international relationships – and indeed our whole understanding of human history and development. For the West, this is quite as radical a change as was ushered in for Europeans by the discovery of the New World. And its impact will become clear more quickly.

There are many obvious differences between China and India. But the prevailing clichés about their differences oversimplify both these countries. It is too easy to define the difference between their development paths as top-down versus bottom-up and then ask which system of government is able to achieve more rapid and more sustainable economic growth.

The contrast is frequently drawn between, on the one hand, India's long tradition of intellectual tolerance, voluble public debate and political pluralism and, on the other hand, a homogenous and centralized China. But this is too simple in a world of increasingly internet-based pluralism. In December 2008, China's online population stood at 290 million – around the same as the total population of the US. With the growth in online users has come a rise in the number of bloggers. The Internet Society of China – a body which represents firms such as service providers, network access carriers and research institutes – estimates the number of bloggers in China at 50 million, and states that 'More and more Chinese want to express their own views about local and international events through the internet.' It is clear that there is plenty of grass-roots vibrancy in the Chinese economy and in its society. Pluralist expression unquestionably impacts on official policy and action. Leonard Woodcock, the first American ambassador in Beijing after the establishment of official relations in 1972, once reflected that, during his lifetime, women in his own country had been denied the vote, labour had not been allowed to organize, and racial discrimination had been legally protected. 'As time passed, we made progress, and I doubt if lectures or threats from foreigners would have moved things faster.' Meanwhile, most Indians recognize – and will typically accept – what they sometimes refer to as the 'democratic discount' in their country's rate of growth compared with that of China.

In other respects too there are differences at one level but similarities which are easier to overlook. China faces a demographic time bomb. Because of the one-child policy, it is often noted that it is the first country in history that will grow old before it grows rich. According to the OECD, births in Beijing, may already be down to 1.4–1.5 per woman; in Shanghai the ratio appears to be 0.96 births per female. The population is ageing, and in 2025 the average age in China will be 40, having been 27 in 1995. In consequence, care of the elderly is clearly becoming a major policy issue in China, given the extent to which most of the country's poor have always depended on working members of their family for support in their old age.

In India, the demographic forecast is in one sense brighter in the near term: birth rates are high, and the average age is coming down. On some estimates, by 2025 it is likely that more than 67 per cent of the total 1.4 billion-strong Indian population will be between 15 and 64 – a potential workforce as much as 36 per cent greater than in 2005. India will then have a lower average age than Europe, the US, Japan or China. This demographic dynamic is likely to make India highly attractive for investment, so long as the challenge of education is met. However, in the longer term, India has to go through a transition to demographic stability of its own. This will not be easy in a country where coercive population control is politically inconceivable and which is already one of the most crowded on the planet.

Both the Indian and the Chinese economies are powerhouses with huge potential. The economic fundamentals of both nations, with their enormous pools of rural labour, point to strong growth for decades ahead. But there are obvious dangers too. The path of economic growth rarely runs smoothly. Financial crashes, coups, political strife, and plain bad management have derailed many other so-called miracle economies, from South East Asia to Latin America. And the same huge populations that can translate into economic power could prove to be a double-edged sword if social, political and environmental challenges are not deftly managed. Both China and India need rapid annual growth to provide jobs for the millions joining the urban workforce each year. Even if India grows at a highly respectable 6.5 per cent a year, it is estimated that there could be an increase of 70 million unemployed by 2012. For similar reasons, Beijing has kept stoking its economy, and the conventional wisdom is that for the foreseeable future China needs growth of above 7 per cent a year on average to create enough urban jobs to absorb migration from the countryside to the cities.

Environmental challenges loom large in both countries. A crucial problem is likely to be water. The two major rivers of both countries have their sources in the ice of a 35,000 km² area of the Himalayas. The strategic scarcity of a resource which most humans have regarded as free for millennia will loom larger and larger in both countries' list of economic development challenges in the next few decades. Also, both countries have paid a steep ecological price for rapid industrial and population growth, with huge numbers of deaths attributed to air and water pollution each year. Air quality in big cities like Chongqing and New Delhi is among the world's worst. And forest cover is vanishing at alarming rates. Enforcement of environmental laws in both nations has been patchy. Many power plants and factories depend on coal and have not invested in clean technologies. Western travellers are often shocked by the resulting pollution. They perhaps forget that their own cities were once like this; photographs of London or Paris fifty years ago would remind them of a time when the civic and cultural monuments they are so familiar with were black with soot.

It is not surprising, therefore, that in both cases there are health concerns too. Both India and China support vast agglomerations of people in their biggest cities. Both are at some risk of epidemics of Aids, tuberculosis and other infectious diseases. And a serious flu epidemic could kill millions in both countries.

None of these challenges is unique to these two huge countries. Indeed, the effects of urbanization are obvious in virtually every emerging economy in the world. The rapid urbanization of the world's population over the twentieth century is measured statistically in the 2007 revision of the UN *World Urbanization Prospects* report. Globally, virtually all future population growth will take place in cities, especially in Asia, Africa and Latin America. By about 2030, four out of five of the world's urban dwellers will live in the developing world's towns and cities. In Asia and Africa, this growth will signal a major shift from rural to urban growth, changing a millennia-long pattern. Globally, the urban population rose from 29 per cent of the total in 1950 to 46 per cent in 2000, and it is predicted to reach 70 per cent – or over 6 billion people – by 2050. From 2008, more than half the people in the world were living in cities.

This urban transformation of the world is the most important social, political and cultural consequence of globalization. In one sense, we are too familiar with it; we need to draw breath and appreciate the sheer enormity of what is happening to the human species. Again, inevitably the statistics are heavily impacted by India and China. India, in the last sixty years, has seen the shift of some 300 million people from villages to cities. In 1947 India's urban population was 60 million; and in 2008 it is estimated to have passed 360 million. It will increase by another 500 million over the next four decades. In percentage terms, there was a rise from 17 per cent urbanization in 1950 to 28 per cent in 2000, and the projected figure for 2050 is 55 per cent.

In China the percentage of people living in cities is growing even more rapidly: from 13 per cent in 1950 to 36 per cent in 2000 to a projected 73 per cent in 2050. It is the largest demographic shift in the history of humankind. And it is worth noting that, by the standards of history, this is a shift which has occurred remarkably smoothly. Compared to the terrible conditions in, say, the Manchester slums in the nineteenth century, where the mortality rate in under-five-year-olds was 50 per cent, or to the horrors of the Soviet Union under Stalin's forced urbanization between the wars, what has happened in China in the last quarter-century is a remarkably peaceful – but no less radical – transformation.

There is some way to go. China is at most halfway through the urbanization process. India is at an even earlier stage. And others are transforming themselves too. Vietnam, for example, was 24 per cent urbanized in 2000, and is heading for 57 per cent by 2050; and in the same time span Bangladesh is moving from 24 per cent to 56 per cent. Urban populations will at least double in every developing region. Everywhere the story is the same – and its political, social, economic, cultural and psychological implications are profound.

Cities embody the drive of humanity for connectedness – for society, convenience, stimulation and wealth. And what do people want when they arrive in these vastly expanding conglomerations of the developing world? When they get the voice and the means what do they ask for? The answer is that they want the same things everywhere: air conditioners, fridges, TVs, mopeds, cars ... If you try to cross the street in Hanoi, there are thousands of mopeds. You stand on the kerb waiting for a gap, but you never get one. So eventually you cross the road anyway, and you find that, lo and behold, they all flow around you like water, but without touching you, and you walk perfectly safely. In Shanghai and in Mumbai the traffic jams are legendary. If either India or China had as many cars per head as there are in the US, it would have as many cars as exist currently on the planet.

But it is not just material conditions that are changing for so many people in so many cities. The social and psychological ramifications of urbanization, too, are profound and global in their impact. The beginnings of academic sociology in the late nineteenth and early twentieth centuries were in many ways influenced by the desire to explain the effects both of commerce and of urbanization on individuals and their social relationships. German sociologists Georg Simmel and Ferdinand Tönnies wrote critical works on individualization and urbanization. As we saw in the last chapter, Simmel focused on how relationships become more and more mediated through money. Tönnies's *Community and Society* (1887) concentrated on the loss of primary relationships such as familial bonds in favour of goal-oriented secondary relationships. Humanity's instinct for commerce and the exchange society lies behind the growth of cities, and as more people enter the global bazaar, urbanization is speeding up. With urbanization comes change to their whole way of viewing the world, bringing both opportunity and discomfort. In cities, some of the streets are paved with gold and others are open sewers. In a lecture entitled *Possible Urban Worlds* (2000), the social theorist David Harvey – Professor of Anthropology at City University, New York – delivered an excoriating assessment of the modern city:

Every city now has its share (often increasing and in some instances predominant) of concentrated impoverishment and human hopelessness, of malnourishment and chronic disease, of crumbling or stressed out infrastructures, of senseless and wasteful consumerism, of ecological degradation and excessive pollution, of congestion, of seemingly stymied economic and human development and of sometimes bitter social strife . . . For many, then, to talk of the city of the twenty-first century is to conjure up a dystopian nightmare in which all that is judged worst in the fatally flawed character of humanity collects together in some hell-hole of despair.

His is an extreme view. But many have analysed the breakdown of security when rural family and village structures give way to urban chaos. Along with the freedoms and potential of individualization come the anxieties of atomization, in which support systems vanish and 'to each his own' becomes both a promise and a threat. The implications for communitarian life, art, government and – ultimately – human fulfilment are profound. And therefore any realistic assessment of progress in the development of the world's emerging economies will inevitably be superficial unless based on a clear recognition of how urbanization will change them to the core.

To see this we have to traverse the history of urbanization, for the roots and differing patterns of the phenomenon tell us a lot. The earliest evidence of true urban settlements dates from around 3000 BC, in ancient Mesopotamia, Egypt and the Indus valley. As cities evolved, they typically displayed both 'organic' and 'planned' types of urban development. These communities had intricate religious, social and military organizations. Separate areas intended for the business of the ruling elite were often highly planned, symmetrical and imposing. These were in sharp contrast to ordinary residential areas, which were generally allowed to grow by a slow and organic process. Two typical features of the ancient city are the wall and the citadel: the wall for defence in regions periodically swept by conquering armies, and the citadel – a large, elevated precinct within the city – devoted to religious and state functions. Cities growing slowly from older settlements were often irregular, adapting gradually to the accidents of topography and history. Colonial cities, however, were sometimes planned before settlement, using a grid system – easy to design, and practical since it parcels land into suitable development plots.

The Romans engaged in extensive city-building in this manner as they consolidated their empire. Rome itself displayed the informal complexity created by centuries of organic growth, although temple and public spaces were highly planned. In contrast, Roman colonial towns built from poor or non-existent bases were very often constructed on a grid pattern or a variation of it. European cities such as

London and Paris arose from these Roman origins. Many Chinese cities too – notably Beijing and Nanjing – were developed on basically similar lines.

However, we usually associate the medieval cities of Europe with narrow winding streets converging on a market square with a cathedral and a city hall. Many cities of this period display this pattern, the product of thousands of incremental additions to the urban fabric, while new towns seeded throughout undeveloped regions of Europe were based upon the familiar grid (Bruges for example). Large encircling walls were built for defence against hostile armies; new walls were built as the city expanded and outgrew its former area. During the Renaissance, architects began to treat the city itself as a piece of architecture that could be given an aesthetically pleasing order. Many of the great public spaces of Italian cities date from this era. With the emergence of great nation states from the seventeenth to the nineteenth century came the baroque city. Ambitious rulers sought the grand scale: long avenues, monumental squares and gardens. Paris, Berlin and Madrid all bear witness to such aspirations – as, in a republican context, does Washington DC.

Towards the latter half of the eighteenth century, however, particularly in America, the city became a setting for commerce. The buildings of the bourgeoisie expanded along with their owners' prosperity: banks, office buildings, warehouses, hotels and small factories. New York, Philadelphia, and Boston around 1920 exemplify the commercial city of this era, with their bustling, mixed-use waterfront districts.

For the first time in a thousand years or more, whole new cities sprang up out of next to nowhere because of industrialization – classic examples are Birmingham in the UK and Essen in Germany, both just tiny villages before the nineteenth century. Shanghai is another example, and a twenty-first century equivalent is Shenzhen (1984 population around 40,000; present population at least 8 million).

It has always been the case, and remains so to this day, that cities act as a magnet or vortex. And the magnet continues to work despite the rapid spread of the internet. Those who expected physical proximity to be rendered redundant by virtual connectivity seem to have been wrong. Today's fastest growing cities have an average annual growth rate of between 4 and 5 per cent – in other words they will double in size in twenty years, if growth continues at that pace. Even to the most travel-worn of world citizen their names are exotic – Behai (China), Ghaziabad (India), Sana'a (Yemen), Surat (India) – to take just the top four from the latest World's Fastest Growing Cities index. The lure of the possible, the promise of the bright lights – they have always exerted a powerful fascination over the human mind.

The early twentieth century excited itself about the megapolis of the future, and drew up plans for it. In 1922 Le Corbusier presented his scheme for a 'Contemporary City' for 3 million inhabitants. With its sixty-storey, cruciform skyscrapers, rectangular park-like green spaces and huge central, multilevel transportation centre – including stations for buses and trains, road intersections and an airport – this was conceptual elegance on an inhuman and artificial scale: the city as machine rather than organism. By contrast, the best current example of a global megalopolis, London, has grown into this role – not assumed it by design. London is the world's purest example of a world city: it is quintessentially organic, open and kaleidoscopic, and constantly growing outwards culturally from its deep roots in the past.

When the Romans invaded Britain in AD 43, they moved north from the Kentish coast and crossed the Thames in the London region – probably at present-day Lambeth – clashing with the local tribesmen just beyond it. Around seven years later they built a permanent wooden bridge, just east of the present London Bridge. This wooden bridge attracted settlers, became a focal point of the Roman road system, and was central to London's subsequent growth. Though the regularity of London's original street grid may indicate that the initial inhabitants were from a military background, trade and commerce soon followed. There were many attractions: among them the fact that the river was deep enough for ships and the surrounding land was relatively well drained, flat and accessible, with plentiful supplies of clay for brick-making. There was soon a flourishing commercial centre.

By the Middle Ages, London had become a maze of twisting streets and lanes. There was little sign left of the Roman military grid. Most of the houses were half-timbered, or wattle and daub, whitewashed with lime. The danger of fire was constant, and laws were passed to make sure that all householders had firefighting equipment on hand. Plague too was a constant threat, because sanitation was so rudimentary. (London was subject to no fewer than sixteen outbreaks of plague between 1348 and the Great Plague of 1665.) City government came under the leadership of the Lord Mayor and council, all of whom were elected from the ranks of the merchant guilds. These guilds ran all the main channels of commerce, amassed huge reserves of wealth, and controlled the city. Each guild had its own hall, and together they had one resplendent meeting place, the Guildhall. There was a real sense in which the city was a law unto itself. Royal power was based upstream at Whitehall, and largely left London to its own devices.

The current vitality of London builds on its historic connections, via immigration and trade, to all the corners of the world. On the corner of Fournier Street and Brick Lane in Spitalfields, just to the east of the City, stands the Jamme Masjid mosque, one of the most striking symbols of the fluidity of London's population. The building has been used for over two and a half centuries as a place of worship for the people of Spitalfields, but the communities assembling within its walls have changed with successive waves of immigration. In 1743, the building started its life as a chapel for the Huguenots who had fled from France in the seventeenth century. In 1819 it became a Wesleyan chapel, but from 1897 the building housed the Spitalfields Great Synagogue, serving the Jewish community who had come to London following pogroms in eastern Europe. Then it became a mosque and was sold to the Bengali community in 1976. Arguably the very word 'refugee' is ingrained in the history of the city: it was coined to describe the Huguenot immigrants seeking refuge from persecution in France.

Britain's borders have historically been open ones; Holbein,

Handel, Brunel, Marx and T. S. Eliot were all immigrants. In 1867, Samuel Smiles referred to London as 'the world's asylum, the refuge of the persecuted of all lands ... one of the most composite populations found in the world'. And an editorial in *The Times* on 19 January 1858 declared that 'every civilized people on the face of the earth must be fully aware that this country is the asylum of nations, and that it would defend the asylum to the last drop of its blood. There is no point on which we are prouder or more resolute [...] we are a nation of refugees.' And most of them came to London.

As a trading centre, too, London reached out to the world, and it has always been sensitive to the winds of change. On the wall of the Court Room at the Bank of England is a dial linked to a weather vane on the building's roof. Knowing the direction of the wind was critical to monetary policy at the time it was installed, in 1805. If the wind was coming from the east, goods would be coming into the London docks and traders would need a plentiful supply of money. Conversely, if a westerly was blowing, the Bank would need to rein in the supply of money to counteract inflationary pressures.

In the late eighteenth century, trade in London gradually assumed the importance (and some of the pomp and circumstance) normally reserved for the Church or the monarchy. The inscription on the West India Dock Foundation Stone needs to be savoured slowly and in full. From the roller coaster of our modern high-speed economy, it is still fleetingly possible to sense from its florid language an older world of moral certainties and optimism about progress, based on industry and commerce:

Of this Range of BUILDINGS
Constructed together with the Adjacent DOCKS. At the Expence of
public spirited individuals
Under the Sanction of the provident Legislature,
And with the liberal Co-operation of the Corporate Body of the
CITY of LONDON
For the distinct Purpose
Of complete SECURITY and ample ACCOMMODATION
(hitherto not afforded)

To the SHIPPING and PRODUCE of the WEST INDIES
at this wealthy PORT
THE FIRST STONE WAS LAID
On Saturday the Twelfth Day of July A.D. 1800
BY THE CONCURRING HANDS OF
THE RIGHT HONOURABLE LORD LOUGHBOROUGH
LORD HIGH CHANCELLOR OF GREAT BRITAIN
THE RIGHT HONOURABLE WILLIAM PITT
FIRST LORD COMMISSIONER OF HIS MAJESTY'S
TREASURY AND CHANCELLOR OF HIS MAJESTY'S
EXCHEQUER
GEORGE HIBBERT Esq., THE CHAIRMAN and ROBERT
MILLIGAN Esq. THE DEPUTY CHAIRMAN
OF THE WEST INDIA DOCK COMPANY
The two former conspicuous in the Band Of those illustrious Statesmen
Who in either House of Parliament have been zealous to promote
The two latter distinguished among those chosen to direct
AN UNDERTAKING
Which, under the favour of GOD, shall contribute
STABILITY, INCREASE and ORNAMENT
TO
BRITISH COMMERCE

Thus trade and finance have always been deeply involved in London's evolution, Indeed, in the boom years of the financial markets in the first part of this decade, London sometimes felt like the very capital of the globalized world. It would be better, though, to describe it as its crossroads. It has some unique advantages – a critical one being the language.

The Oxford English Dictionary includes over 600,000 definitions, and many of them for words borrowed from other languages. The things that define London are also largely true of the language. More than ever before in the history of the world, English can now be called the lingua franca of the modern era: it is the primary language in more than thirty-five countries, and an official language (but not necessarily the most widely spoken) in at least thirty-five others. It is the world's leading second language, and is rapidly absorbing aspects of cultures worldwide as it continues to grow. It has borrowed more words from more languages than any other language. It is, by international treaty, the official language for aerial and maritime communications, and an official language of the United Nations and of virtually all other international organizations. The 'General Explanations' at the beginning of *The Oxford English Dictionary* state, 'The vocabulary of a widely diffused and highly cultivated living language is not a fixed quantity circumscribed by definite limits ... there is absolutely no defining line in any direction: the circle of the English language has a well-defined centre but no discernible circumference.'

There are other factors too that make London such an unusual crossroads – political stability, its legal system, its open markets and, as much as anything, its geographical position in the time zones: London is on the Prime Meridian. From London it is possible to work a normal day and talk to Tokyo in the morning and Los Angeles in the afternoon. One way and another, and without a conscious strategy, over the past twenty-five years London has turned itself into an international marketplace. People have flocked to it from every corner of the world and in every socio-economic bracket. Over 30 per cent of London residents were born outside the country, and there are 33 different communities consisting of more than 10,000 people born outside the country.

And so London has become a cultural – as well as commercial – crossroads of the world. More than 275 languages are regularly spoken in the city. The diversity of influences and traditions has shaped the city's culture into what it is today. The city is an international centre for arts, music, festivals, museums and much more. Just one example of many: the British Museum is the world's largest museum of human history, culture and art. Every cuisine in the world can now be found in London – even British cuisine has managed to shed its unappealing image and can be found in expensive and fashionable restaurants.

*

True world cities today are still few – arguably just London, New York and Paris. But what is it that makes a great world city? The key characteristics surely include active influence on and participation in international events and world affairs; a large population including significant international communities; major travel, communications and financial hubs; world-renowned cultural institutions and universities; a lively cultural scene, including arts festivals, theatre and opera; powerful and influential media with international reach; and strong sporting interests, including world-class sports facilities able to host major international events. If these are the ingredients that make for a world city, then the next few generations will see other world cities emerge in Asia and elsewhere.

But such world cities are only the apex of urbanization. Much more generally, it is as if the human experience of urbanization is changing consciousness itself. Urbanization seems to embody Teilhard de Chardin's ideas: in his world view, as evolution progresses, so there is a continual increase of both complexity and consciousness. For Teilhard the socialization of humankind is a crucial stage of this process. The finite and spherical surface of the earth contributes to the increased compaction and socialization of humankind and to the emergence of the noosphere. Urbanization is arguably the quintessential manifestation of this process. The ambiguity of its effects on human beings mirrors Teilhard's ambivalence about the process itself.

Put another way, when people get together in cities and form countless intricate webs, they seem to acquire a new life force; they become more unpredictable, uncontrollable and powerful than the stable communities of settled rural life. Cities tend to be hotbeds of popular movement, and hard for authorities to deal with. The Romans, from early on, understood the power of the people of the city. The initials 'SPQR' that still appear all over Roman imperial buildings, from the Latin 'Senatus Populusque Romanus' ('the Senate and Roman People'), were a standing reminder that authority depended on at least the acquiescence of the people. Government of all kinds – absolutist, centralist, democratic – has been reminded of this time and again down the ages. One of the best examples of a city with a life of its own, with a people power that often erupts on to the streets to traumatize the politicians and rulers, is Paris. Few centuries have gone by without their share of Parisian upheavals; from the Hundred Years War, to the nineteenth-century barricades, through to present times.

Adolf Hitler always hated Berlin, a city which never produced a majority for the Nazis and which stood for everything he loathed. (The feeling was mutual.) In his 2002 biography *Hitler*, Joachim Fest describes the leader's antipathy:

The hectic madness of Berlin, which was then entering its famous, or notorious, twenties, only heightened Hitler's dislike of the city. He despised its greed and its frivolity, comparing conditions there with those of declining Rome in the Late Empire. There, too, he said, 'racially alien Christianity' had taken advantage of the city's weakness, as Bolshevism today was battening on the moral decay of Germany. The speeches of those early years are full of attacks upon metropolitan vice, corruption, and excess, as he had observed them on the glittering pavements of Friedrichstrasse or the Kurfuerstendamm.

Cities, in short, have always represented a challenge to official power. Why? Not just because of the logistical difficulties of controlling large mobs in confined spaces (a consideration which famously lay behind Haussmann's remodelling of Paris in the 1860s). More fundamentally, it is because of the challenge they represent to any form of settled social structure. They are natural cauldrons of atomization – constantly tending to break down pre-existing structures and allowing new relationships to form and then re-form. It is this atomization which led to the preoccupation amongst sociologists and in literature with that very modern human condition – alienation.

In critical social theory, 'alienation' refers to an individual's estrangement from 'the other' – from traditional community, from our environment, from others in general. For Marx, alienation was a systematic result of capitalism, in which what naturally belongs together is forced apart, and what is properly in harmony is set in antagonistic tension. People are alienated from essential aspects of their own human nature. For Marx, economic conditions lay at the root of this disorder: under the conditions of capitalistic industrial production, workers inevitably lose control of their lives and selves, since they have no control over their work. Workers never become autonomous, self-realized human beings in any individualized sense. Alienation in capitalist societies occurs because work no longer takes place in and around the cottage, but in regimented factories where people are made to work for almost all their waking hours and for wages that are as low as the capitalist owner can get away with. So old structures are destroyed. The new structures alienate. This for Marx was the essence of urban commercial and capitalist life.

For Simmel, the metropolis was a place which altered how the individual interacted with other individuals. Differently from Marx, he focused on how the individualization made possible by the city created alienation. The atomism of modern urban society means that individuals have an ever wider range of ever shallower relations with other people. The result, eventually, is the notorious loneliness in the crowd that cities make possible. The growth of the city, and the brevity and scarcity of the inter-human contacts of the metropolitan dweller, as compared to the stable social intercourse of the rural community, meant that individual self-awareness became a private matter as never before. In more integrated, pre-urban societies, individual self-awareness is a shared, socially shaped personality. But in urban experience individuals come to perceive themselves as 'other than' the relationship they have with their environment – thus posing for the individual the question of how to react to this reality 'out there'. The question can be psychologically liberating, but also unsettling.

From this follows an increasingly urgent psychological drive for self-actualization which manifests itself in the celebration of activity. Abraham Maslow, in his famous 1943 article 'A Theory of Human Motivation', defined self-actualization as 'the desire to become more and more what one is, to become everything that one is capable of becoming'. He believed that people who achieve self-actualization are characterized by certain behaviour patterns. Common traits include embracing reality and facts rather than denial, being spontaneous, having an interest in solving problems, and accepting oneself and others without prejudice. These look remarkably like key factors for success in the open, fluid environment of city life.

Self-actualization in this sense is the response of privatized self-awareness to what Simmel called the 'objective culture' of the city. In Simmel's view, social interaction – designed to elicit recognition, or at least awareness, from others – became an essential aspect of the individual response to alienation; it became another means of self-actualization, and would inevitably often take aggressive forms. In urban life, this becomes an existential imperative such as it never is in a more stable integrated rural life. It would be wrong, however, to see this in purely – or even primarily – negative terms. Simmel also argued, for example, that another manifestation of this essentially urban drive is romanticism. This might seem counter-intuitive. However, he saw it as no coincidence that romanticism, with its celebration of the experience of nature, flourishes as cultures become urbanized. As Simmel puts it in *The Philosophy of Money*:

To be sure the distinctive aesthetic and romantic experience of nature is perhaps possible only through this process [of becoming remote from nature]. Whoever lives in direct contact with nature and knows no other form of life may enjoy its charm subjectively, but he lacks that distance from nature that is the basis for aesthetic contemplation and the root of that quiet sorrow, that feeling of yearning estrangement and of a lost paradise that characterizes the romantic response to nature.

For example, consider the semi-mystical contemplation of cherry blossom that goes on every year in urbanized, crowded Japan. Or the enduring popularity of Pushkin and Shishkin in Russia; or of Constable and Elgar in England – all of them analogous yearnings of urbanized cultures. Simmel could have generalized the point: he might have argued that – to use his own terminology – the emergence of the objective culture as something 'over and against' the individual was a fundamental reason why art generally is so much a product of urban life. Art requires distance – psychological distance – from 'the other', not just from nature, as the basis for aesthetic contemplation.

Self-actualization in urban culture can take other forms too, of course. One, characteristic of mid-twentieth-century European literature, is existentialism. In Albert Camus's existentialist novel *The Stranger* (1942), the bored, alienated protagonist, Meursault, struggles to construct an individual system of values as he responds to the disappearance of the old ones. He lives in a state of anomie – the complete loss of belief and purpose – which pervades the book from the opening line: 'Today mother died. Or maybe yesterday, I don't know.' When Meursault is prosecuted for shooting an Arab man during a fight, the prosecuting attorneys seem more interested in the inability or unwillingness of Meursault to cry at his mother's funeral than in the murder of the Arab, because they find his lack of sorrow offensive. The novel ends with Meursault (defiantly?) recognizing the universe's 'sublime indifference' toward humankind. Meursault emerges at the start of the novel as a blunt and unfeeling individual. Ultimately, he accepts the world as essentially meaningless, such that the only way to arrive at any purpose is to make it for oneself. A very urban instinct.

Hermann Hesse's *Steppenwolf* (1927) is another classic existentialist text. The 'wolf from the steppes' is in fact a middle-aged man named Harry Haller, who is beset with reflections on his being ill-suited for the world of 'everybody', the regular people. He is given a book which describes the two natures of man: one 'high', spiritual and 'human'; the other 'low' and animal-like. Humanity, it seems, is cursed with perpetual discontent as it struggles blindly between one nature and the other, blind to any alternative possibilities. While Haller longs to break free, he in fact continues to live utterly conventionally as a bourgeois bachelor. He holds that the people of the Dark Ages did not suffer more than those of (an idealized) classical antiquity. It is those who are trapped between the two who suffer the most. It is hard to find a more striking image of the dilemma of individualization which is the essence of urban life than this wolf from the steppes imprisoned inside the bourgeois bachelor.

*

What then does this all amount to? We live in a globalizing, urbanizing world. Can this be the New Jerusalem? Certainly one line of thinking – the one that culminates in Fukuyama's ending of history or Friedman's 'flat' world – would suggest that it is, or at least could be. The human trading instinct first emerged thousands of years ago, and subsequently underpinned the connections, empires, technologies, luxuries and culture of the modern world. Those trading instincts have led us into a world which even to our recent ancestors would have been a world of unimaginable privilege: a world where the individual freedom to transcend the bonds of poverty, ignorance, disease, psychological entrapment and social insignificance means that, for example, the Hawaii-born son of a Kenyan can dream of becoming a world-changer; a world where people increasingly gather in great cities of millions or more in which every human luxury and need is available within half an hour to those can afford it; a world where friends and families can remain connected even when separated by tens of thousands of miles for year after year; and a world where love can blossom between people of different languages and cultures as never before in history.

Or is this only half the picture, and a very rose-tinted one at that? Is the truth not much more frightening: a picture of humanity sleepwalking to disaster, dazed and drugged by its own self-indulgence? For we know how globalization and urbanization have also created huge consumption of increasingly scarce global resources; how humanity must face the possibility that it may be living on an unsustainable scale, which could see future generations gravely threatened; how bitter poverty still shackles hundreds of millions of people to brief lives of suffering and hopelessness; how the gap between these people and the wealthiest has got wider; how for even the majority who live in relative luxury there is a price to pay for fast cars and flat-screen televisions, the price of loneliness and nagging fear that it may all amount to nothing; and how there are still deep clashes between world views that stubbornly resist reasoned debate and inspire the suicide bombers and terror networks of the twenty-first century.

Is this progress? If so, it is certainly ambiguous progress. The development momentum is obvious – in the statistics, and to the astonished naked eye in so much of the developing world. Yet urbanization is so big a change, and so recent, that it is hard to grasp just how much it will change who we are. Individualization and social liberation are inextricably entwined with it. They seem to be goods facilitating self-actualization on a broader scale than ever before; yet they have an obvious shadow side.

Two hundred years before 1989 and the putative 'end of history', the French Revolution shook the Western world. This was one of the biggest political earthquakes of the whole of human history. It unleashed a quarter of a century of war in Europe; political turbulence which reverberated through the nineteenth and twentieth centuries; and controversy about human rights, the nature of society and the role of the state, the aftershocks of which are with us to this day. Wiser by far than those who thought of 1989 as the end of history was Zhou Enlai. When asked what were the consequences of the French Revolution, he replied, 'It is too soon to tell.' And it is certainly too soon to assess an urban revolution of the whole species which is still in train.

What we know is that we fret about what is happening to us – whether we are rich or poor. In particular, as the first decade of a new century nears its close amid a financial and economic crisis which is the worst for nearly eighty years, globalized market capitalism is in the dock as it has not been for a generation. Wherever we are, this is certainly not the New Jerusalem. As we reflect on where we seem to be heading, we agonize – perhaps increasingly as economic difficulties deepen – over four key series of questions: (i) Is open-market capitalism – the engine of global growth for a generation – intrinsically unstable? If so, what should we do about it, and how should we police human commerce? (ii) What of the marginalized, both within fast-growing and mature economies and also those whole countries which have been left behind by globalization and remain mired in poverty? (iii) Can a finite planet cope? How long can humanity continue to consume resources at the level we currently do? (iv) Where does individualization lead? If everything has a price, what does this do to our sense of value? Of rights and duties? Of belonging? Of who we are?

These are the questions for the next three chapters

5

From Tulips to Sub-Prime to . . .

Nobody knew with the least precision what Mr Merdle's business was, except that it was to coin money.
                              Charles Dickens, *Little Dorrit* (1857)

Speculators may do no harm as bubbles on a steady stream of enterprise. But the position is serious when enterprise becomes the bubble on a whirlpool of speculation. When the capital development of a country becomes a by-product of the activities of a casino, the job is likely to be ill-done.
                              John Maynard Keynes, *The General Theory of Employment, Interest and Money* (1936)

Thus the whirligig of time brings in his revenges.
                              William Shakespeare, *Twelfth Night* (1601)

In late January 2009 the World Economic Forum met as usual in Davos. The theme, 'Shaping the Post-Crisis world', was either optimistic or long-range, since at that stage it was by no means clear when the world would emerge from crisis. The summing-up message from the Forum was that global leaders must develop a swift and coordinated response to the most serious global recession since the 1930s. This was predictable rhetoric: the world's leaders riding to the rescue of the world's people.

Behind the elegant words, during the Forum there had been pointed criticism of the Western-inspired capitalist model which had so conspicuously broken down. After years of criticism by Western economists for the sins of state interference and 'crony capitalism', Asian policymakers felt justified in hitting back. Now it was the turn of the West to take correction, for its credit-fuelled asset-bubble and its painfully imploding growth model.

China's premier, Wen Jiabao, pilloried Western banks for their 'blind pursuit of profit and lack of discipline' and, quoting Adam Smith, scolded the former high priests of untrammelled capitalism for their 'unsustainable model of development characterized by prolonged low savings and high consumption'.

Other voices chimed in alongside him. One, Prakash Javadekar, from India's Bharatiya Janata Party, described Western capitalism as 'nothing but overindulgence'. Eisuke Sakakibara, a former senior Japanese finance official, predicted, 'The American age is over.' Kishore Mahbubani, dean of Singapore's Lee Kuan Yew School of Public Policy, said Asians had learned some valuable lessons from watching mistaken Western excess: 'Do not liberalize the financial sector too quickly, borrow in moderation, save in earnest, take care of the real economy, invest in productivity, focus on education.' The critics had a phrase for the Western overindulgence that they were attacking: 'casino capitalism.'

'Casino capitalism' was a phrase popularized in 1986 by Susan Strange, Professor of International Relations at the London School of Economics from 1978 to 1988. It was the title of what became her best-known book. In it, she warned about how the speed at which markets work, combined with their near-universal reach, would result in levels of global volatility that had never been experienced before. In a world where the vast bulk of market trading has no direct relation to any real business requirement, what concerned her was how the instability of active markets could devalue the economic base of real lives or, in macroeconomic terms, could lead to the collapse of national and regional economies. She focused particularly on innovations in the way in which financial markets work; the sheer size of markets, the trend for commercial banks to expand into investment banking, and the deregulation of the markets.

'Casino capitalism' brought other, less purely economic, troubles in its wake. The fraudster has always been drawn to the casino, and the liberalized financial markets with their ability to create sudden geysers of cash inevitably attracted the attention of manipulators and crooks. Even those who have not seen Michael Douglas's Oscar-winning performance in Oliver Stone's 1987 film *Wall Street* will know the approximate meaning of 'pump and dump' and 'short and distort', and will be familiar with the caricature of the ruthless, amoral city banker making millions from dubious transactions. And those who remember the arbitrageurs, the corporate raiders and the junk-bond kings of the 1980s will know that, like any good caricature, Douglas's role was based on close observation of reality. Even then, the barbarians were at the gates; in the twenty years or so since then, the gates seem to have been opened wide.

So it is not surprising that the financial markets and their way-wardness – their upheavals, distortions, manipulations – have caused intense and widespread anger; or that we ask ourselves if globalization is allowing them to get completely out of hand. It is not surprising that we ask whether they will eventually blow up in a way which permanently damages economic and social well-being. Or that we ask, Why should ordinary people suffer from all this destructive excess?

The global economic crisis that began in 2007 has been the deepest, broadest and most dangerous financial crisis since 1929. It may even come to rank as one of the great turning points in the history of the modern world – as a time with epoch-moulding consequences. We are too close to it to be certain of this, of course, let alone to have a clear view of what its consequences will be. But at the very least, as the head of America's National Economic Council, Lawrence Summers – a strong defender of free markets – concluded in the spring of 2009, the belief that the market is inherently self-stabilizing, always, has been 'dealt a fatal blow ... it is wrong a few times a century and this is one of those times.'

For a while, the scale of what was happening was not fully apparent. When the storm broke, in the summer of 2007, many hoped that the worst would be over by Christmas (rather as the European powers in August 1914 had thought the war would be over by Christmas), or at least by the spring or the summer of 2008. In fact it was to grow into something far worse – a hurricane unprecedented in its savagery.

The scope of the financial crisis was shocking, affecting the global economy deeply in every area, causing the tightening of credit, stock-exchange declines, liquidity problems in equity and hedge funds, devaluation of assets underpinning pension funds and insurance contracts, massively increasing public debt, and spreading currency volatility. To many it felt as though the crisis had come out of a clear blue sky – leaving, for instance, Alan Greenspan, chairman of the US Federal Reserve from 1987 to 2006, 'in a state of shocked disbelief'.

But there were warning signs, and the first breezes of the oncoming hurricane were perhaps detectable as early as 2005. It is all too easy from today's vantage point to pick out the forecasts that were un-cannily correct and to ignore the consensus that was too optimistic. But there was in fact a growing concern amongst economists and financiers that the world's markets were looking increasingly stretched – and a growing sense that at some point the music would stop.

By the end of 2005, more and more economists were pointing out that America was living beyond its means. It was by then the world's biggest debtor country, and US consumers saved virtually nothing. Meanwhile, the fiscal position had deteriorated dramatically. The Bush administration had cut taxes while spending vast sums in Iraq. The US economy was dependent upon the reserves of Japan, China and others being invested in US Treasury bonds to fund the fiscal and current-account deficits. Low interest rates kept American consumers active, and the economy grew robustly. But it was unbalanced, and economists were not slow to point this out. None-theless, very few indeed imagined how savage the correction would be when it finally came.

Below the surface lay a more fundamental shift in the world's economic centre of gravity – a trend which was established well before 2007, and which will continue over the next generation and beyond. This shift has not been halted by the current crisis: in fact the crisis will accelerate it. There is a much wider dynamic at work that will change the world economy as much in the next half century as it has changed in the last.

For the last two hundred years the world's economic centre of gravity has been centred on Western economies, latterly the US in particular. The G7 today still generates over half of the world's output, although it has only a seventh of its population. But from 1990 the economic hegemony of the older industrialized world has been increasingly challenged by the rise of developing economies, especially in Asia – and, within Asia, particularly by the world's two largest countries, China and India. The mushrooming of these economies has created what can perhaps be described as a macro-economic rectangle. The rectangle is made up of, on one side, consuming nations – in particular the US (which has become what might be termed the world's consumer of last resort), but also countries such as the UK and a number of other European economies. On another side of the rectangle there are what might be called the 'workshop nations' – mainly the fast-growth emerging economies, which have been manufacturing a vast range of goods for consumption in the West. On a third side are the resource providers – those economies whose wealth of hydrocarbons and other commodities has fuelled the production of the workshops and has therefore commanded such high prices in recent years. And finally, on a fourth side, there are two major capital-goods exporters which have equipped the workshops (Japan and Germany).

This rectangle delivered very strong global growth in the last decade, but it was inherently unstable, and it has given rise to the financial imbalances that lie at the heart of the present crisis. The workshop nations, the resource providers and the capital-goods exporters have accumulated massive savings, the vast bulk of which have been invested in the world's reserve currency, the US dollar. This investment had profound consequences. Yields in the government bond markets were significantly reduced as they drew in the surplus liquidity from emerging markets (over 50 per cent of US Treasury debt is now owned by foreign investors, with China overtaking Japan in 2008 as the single largest holder). This decline in yield prompted investors to look for alternatives which seemed to fit the requirement of higher yields with – apparently – limited risk. Mortgage-backed securities were the obvious choice: those securities were liquid, and were backed by mortgages on people's homes. This stimulated huge growth in the issuance of these securities: in 1990, just 10 per cent of mortgages in the United States were securitized – repackaged into bonds – but by 2007 this had risen to over 70 per cent. This in turn permitted a massive growth in total mortgage lending – far more than the lenders could ever have financed from their own balance sheets.

The combination of a tidal wave of liquidity and the search for yield meant that the ratio of risk to return began to rise. The overall result was a boom in house prices and a binge of consumer borrowing. By any measure, Western consumer economies were becoming very highly geared, relying heavily on borrowing. In the US, the ratio of household debt to GDP rose sharply – to 100 per cent in 2007, from 66 per cent ten years earlier. By the summer of 2008, the UK's overall household debt had reached 109 per cent of GDP – the highest in the G7.

Loose monetary conditions in the US and in much of the emerging world gave added potency to this already lethal cocktail. Following the bursting of the dot-com bubble in 2000, the terrorist attacks of 11 September 2001 and the consequent stock market falls, the US Federal Reserve reacted by sharply lowering short-term interest rates in order to head off a downturn in economic activity, and it held them low for an unusually long period. This loosened the money supply not only in the US but in other economies around the world which habitually manage their currency against the dollar – including many of the world's fastest growing emerging markets. So when the US held interest rates low, the result was lower monetary conditions not just in the US but also in many parts of the emerging world as well.

As the consumer was gearing up, so were the banks. In the US, the aggregate debt of the financial sector rose from 22 per cent of GDP in 1981 to 117 per cent by the third quarter of 2008. In the UK, the gross debt of the financial sector reached almost 250 per cent of GDP. In the Western financial system as a whole, leverage/ gearing increased rapidly, both directly and indirectly – directly, in that bank balance sheets became more and more highly geared; and indirectly, in that the banks packaged and sold securitized assets (often with mortgages as the underlying source of value) to investors around the world. Securitized assets – mortgages and other loans repackaged into bonds – had been in existence since the 1980s. What changed was the huge growth in volume and a spectacular increase in the complexity of the financial engineering used to create new investment vehicles for those looking for a good yield on what appeared to be safe assets. The result was that the first decade of the new century saw the mushrooming of a complex web of so-called structured finance around the world.

Another sign of the growing complexity of these financial inter-relationships was that in one decade the gross value of financial derivatives leaped by a factor of four. The structuring and securitiza-tion that all this financial engineering made possible resulted in the diffusion of risk to investors around the world – which meant that lenders could create more mortgages and other loans for each dollar of capital than they could before. And that, in turn, meant three things: first, that lenders could easily be tempted into overlending and therefore inflating asset bubbles to bursting point; second, that the transfer of risk could make it very difficult to see who was ultimately the bearer of the loss in the case of a credit collapse; and, third, the complexity of the structures could make it extremely unclear what their real value was in the event of credit difficulties in the underlying asset. (It is all this that gives rise to the problem of what have become popularly known as 'toxic assets'.) Gillian Tett of the *Financial Times* memorably described all this as 'candyfloss' money – akin to the way a small amount of sugar can be spun into a huge cone of candyfloss.

Behind it all, and compounding the dangers, lay a market pre-disposition to overconfidence. For years the West had been enjoying what was dubbed 'the Goldilocks economy'. It was called this because it was deemed to be, so to speak, neither too hot nor too cold but just right – though the connotations of its being a fairy tale later turned out to be relevant too. Countries like the US and Britain, so it was said, could go on eating all the porridge produced by China for ever. The markets had made it possible to achieve strong growth without the risk of inflation and overheating. Business cycles were a thing of the past, it seemed.

To make matters yet more perilous, even the risk managers were too often coming to believe in their own invulnerability. 'The golden age of risk management' was a phrase used by some to describe a financial system in which risk-measurement models were so sophisticated that they would remove more uncertainty than ever before from the tricky business of making profits from finance. At the heart of this belief was the widespread assumption that the markets would always be liquid enough to allow any financial instrument to be bought or sold readily. What was measurable seemed manageable; and what was manageable must be comfortable. In this so-called golden age, banks and investors systematized the risk by the use of sophisticated models whose ultimate purpose was to price debt – the trouble being that no one predicted how rapidly the models would fall apart if confidence broke down and the financial markets became very illiquid. Thus the golden age was in fact an undermanaged age, because not enough people understood the models and their limitations, and because the immediate rewards were simply too large to be forgone: all boats floated as the tide came in.

'The perfect storm' is a phrase so often used that its origins are sometimes forgotten – it was the title of an investigative book published in 1997 by Sebastian Junger about the 1991 Halloween nor'easter that sunk the fishing boat *Andrea Gail* and devastated the lives of many American fishing and sailing families. The title arose from Junger's interviews with meteorologists about the weather patterns building up to the storm. They said this was a storm in which all the ingredients were as bad as they could be – if a computer had designed the worst storm imaginable, it could not have done better. It would be wrong to call the financial crisis that began in 2007 'the perfect crisis', since it could certainly have been immeasurably worse. And yet what is clear as one reviews the crisis even from a little distance in time is just how many forces simultaneously fed into the same destructive vortex.

We have touched upon some: the massive financial imbalances caused by macroeconomic relationships; a sustained global period of loose money; a fundamental complacency both macroeconomic, institutional and individual; a financial system which was over-confident in its own risk-management techniques; the globalizing of the bubble through securitization and the widespread dispersion of risk. Economic historians will surely study this period for many years to come.

And, as often with storms, there was something of a heavy calm before it. False calm, certainly; and followed by a series of events of breathtaking savagery.

Why was the storm, when it finally burst, so unexpectedly severe? By early 2007 the signs were pretty clear: everything looked stretched – not just mortgages, but other financial markets such as those in leveraged loans. Property markets were slowing down in the US, Britain and elsewhere, and fears of an end to the Goldilocks economy were rising (though inflation seemed as great a risk as recession).

The world's finances certainly seemed stretched – and yet they were underpinned by large pools of liquidity. Asian and Middle Eastern sovereign wealth funds were flush with investable money. The foreign-exchange reserves of the major developing-economy exporters were rising month by month. The global private equity market was booming; 2007 was a record year for fund-raising. There was nervousness, certainly, but liquidity seemed limitless.

The International Monetary Fund's official forecast published in April 2007 captured the prevailing thinking of the time. 'It may surprise readers to learn that this *World Economic Outlook* sees global economic risks as having *declined* since our last issue in September 2006,' began the second paragraph of the foreword. The report went on to predict the 'continuation of strong global growth' despite worrying news from the US housing market and a slowing of growth in the US. Among positive signs, the IMF noted a strong US labour market. Elsewhere, it pointed to the fastest growth in six years in the euro area, increased momentum in Japan, and remarkable growth in China and India. During the five-year period 2003–7, it reminded readers, the global economy was achieving its fastest pace of sustained growth since the early 1970s. Yet five months later there would be no doubt in anyone's mind: the unthinkable was happening.

In fact the poison was already spreading through the system when the IMF forecast appeared. In the spring of 2007 the mortgage-securitization markets started to dry up. By the autumn of 2008 they were nearly shut down altogether – meaning that about a third of the private-credit markets thus became unavailable as a source of funds. And the market had turned. By September 2008 average US house prices had fallen by over 20 per cent from their mid-2006 peak. The signs of pain were becoming all too obvious from 2007 onward as the number of foreclosures rose, and as banks had to take large write-downs on the value of mortgage-backed securities still on their books.

Fear began to spread through the financial markets. In the autumn of 2007 it looked as if the interbank funding markets were seizing up. Banks had drastically curtailed lending to each other, as they mistrusted each other's balance sheets. The financial system, as someone said at the time, increasingly resembled a football team each of whose players refused to pass the ball to his teammates for fear of not receiving it back.

For the banking system, funding problems are deadly; they can kill banks more quickly than capital shortages. Central banks worked to stave off a complete collapse of the global banking system with massive injections of cash into money markets in coordinated efforts to ease conditions.

Banks and other lenders began to fail, both in the US and in Europe. In September 2007, pictures of people in orderly queues outside branches of the Northern Rock Bank in the UK evoked folk memories around the world of bank runs of earlier times. And by the second half of 2008 the world's news seemed to be dominated by bailouts, recapitalizations and bankruptcies.

The pivotal event occurred on Sunday 14 September 2008, when Lehman Brothers announced it would file for bankruptcy – the largest bankruptcy in US history. This dealt a body blow to a financial system already gravely weakened by over twelve months of increasing stress. Until then, creditors' confidence in the stability of the system had perhaps been strong enough to ascribe individual failures to specific issues arising from, for example, the drying-up of the securitization market. But from that moment on the fear grew that the entire financial system might collapse.

What would collapse of the system mean? Bank closures, countless businesses and individuals denied access to their savings or to credit – leading to business failures, unemployment, widespread social distress, panic. Shades, in fact, of the 1930s. And the fear was no respecter of borders, as it spread round the world like the medieval plague.

By now the financial crisis was also gravely weakening the economy, and almost no country was spared. This was not only the first major financial crisis of the globalized securitization era: it was also the first crisis of the global 'just-in-time' economy. The philosophy of just-in-time is about having 'the right material, at the right time, at the right place, and in the exact amount', without the safety buffer of warehouses full of reserve supplies. Just-in-time management was mooted by Henry Ford in the early 1920s, and was refined and rigorously applied by Toyota from the 1950s onward. Today it is increasingly a global practice and a *sine qua non* of successful manufacturing. But it had two major effects on the consequences of the crisis which began in 2007.

First, it meant that there was no elasticity in the system. The shock waves from the financial earthquake's epicentre jarred manufacturing with unprecedented immediacy in a way that few really foresaw. In sector after sector, business people were quite suddenly recounting stories of empty order books. This was not just the case in retailing, where it might perhaps have been expected, but also in chemicals, construction, engineering, steel, plastics, aerospace and more. Hardly any sector was unscathed.

Second, it spread the shock waves globally in parallel to the financial shock, through supply chains which had become globalized as in Thomas Friedman's famous example of his Dell laptop. So, while banks all over the world were staggering because of the collapse of financial asset values, manufacturing supply chains transmitted the ferocity of the downturn in the economy all round the world with unprecedented speed.

And the sudden weakening of the economy fed through in turn to the commodity markets and into capital goods exports. All four sides of the rectangle were thus impacted. Oil prices, for example, fell in four months to less than a quarter of their peak price: from a record of $147 a barrel on 11 July 2008 to a low of $34 on 21 December 2008. As a result, in countries like Saudi Arabia and Kuwait, where oil provides 90 per cent of the national income, there were concerns – the first for many years – about balancing national budgets.

In the spring of 2009 the International Monetary Fund, striking a very different tone from two years before, warned of deep recessions in all advanced economies and blamed the 'mutually reinforcing negative feedback loop' between the 'corrosive' financial sector and the stalling economy. This had intensified, it said, and prospects for recovery before mid-2010 were receding. In October 2008 the Bank of England had already warned that the credit crisis was beginning to impact on the economy. Britain faced the prospect, it said, of large numbers of British companies failing through credit starvation. Its regular survey of credit conditions showed that there had been a sharp reduction in the availability of credit to companies over the previous three months, as part of a vicious circle in which banks cut lending to companies in response to the downturn, thus weakening the balance sheets of the companies.

Unemployment was rising. Labour-market projections for 2009 reinforced the general mood of pessimism, forecasting an unemployment increase globally of anything between 20 million and 50 million people. There was a rising tide of warnings about a repetition of the 'financial dance of death' of the 1930s: falling incomes, rising unemployment, and the rising real burden of debt.

And unquestionably there were some uncomfortable parallels between the events of 1929–32 and of 2007–9. The Great Depression had also resulted from a slump in the value of assets held by the banks, which then drained the lifeblood from the economy. It too was not just made in America – it had spread internationally, and had cried out for international cooperation to remedy it.

But government actions and inaction had turned the crisis of 1929 into an international catastrophe. The worst government measure – indeed, one of the worst pieces of economic legislation of the entire century – had been the Smoot–Hawley Tariff Act passed by the United States Congress in 1930, and not vetoed by President Hoover despite an avalanche of protests from economists at its raising tariffs to record levels on over 20,000 imported goods. But governments also tightened monetary conditions and sought to balance their budgets. Elsewhere, inaction ruled the day. Banks failed on both sides of the Atlantic, but the response was disorganized, paralysed by ideological debate, and hopelessly inadequate.* The Fed went into paralysis. In February 1931 its Open Market Committee did not meet at all. In the end, in response to the spreading crisis of confidence, President Roosevelt had to take the drastic step of shutting every bank in America for more than a week.

In the 1930s, no country was willing to take the lead. Britain had been the pre-eminent financial power up until the First World War. By 1929 it was incapable of leadership, while the US – still hesitant on the world stage – was unwilling to lead. And when larger groups of countries were assembled to treat the problem, they turned out to be ineffectual. The London Economic Conference of June 1933, at which representatives of sixty-six nations met to attack global depression, revive international trade, and stabilize international currencies, collapsed ignominiously.

The response to the crisis of 2007–9 has, by contrast, been hectically proactive. 'We are all Keynesians now' has been the watchword. Milton Friedman coined the phrase in 1965; President Nixon popularized it years later when the Bretton Woods agreement that regulated the international monetary system broke down at the beginning of the 1970s. Keynesianism then went out of fashion in the new free-market oriented consensus of the post-Thatcher/Reagan

*Tony Jackson describes this at greater length in 'Parallels with 1929 Highlight Need for Radical Thinking', *Financial Times*, 5 October 2008.

era. But the crisis brought it back into vogue, and by the summer of 2008 it was taken up with very little hesitation, even by those who were concerned about the longer term effects on public finances.

This Keynesian recognition that, rather than let the free market take its course, it was necessary for governments to stabilize economies suffering from a lack of demand by stepping in with tax cuts and/or public-expenditure increases was a reversal of the orthodoxy of the previous two decades. The Keynesian consensus became clear in November 2008 in a G20 communiqué vowing to 'use fiscal measures to stimulate domestic demand to rapid effect'. The US, the UK, China, Japan and Korea all became energetic and vocal proponents of fiscal stimulus. And as interest rates had been reduced to close to zero, central banks also turned to their weapon of last resort – quantitative easing, a practice which enabled them to pump money into the markets by buying up bonds, mortgages and other assets. Many predicted that the next challenge – given all this largesse – would be a resurgence of inflation a few years down the line: but virtually everyone agreed that the risk of inflation later was less threatening than the risk of deflation now.

And the world held its breath (and felt exhausted: when the history books are written about this period, I believe they will miss an important dimension if they do not focus on the pervasive stress and the sheer tiredness of those involved – whether policymakers, regulators or bankers). How would consumers respond to this massive exercise in economic artificial respiration? Would trade and investment reconnect? How soon would inflation rear its head again? How severe would the setback for the emerging markets be? And what were the implications for geopolitics?

Whatever the answer, it was clear that a fundamental conflict was being played out. This stemmed from the tension between the short-term imperative to minimize recession and the long-term need to adjust to a world that would be very different. In the short term, the case for adopting Keynesian measures to pump-prime the economy, cope with recession, and stave off something far worse was compelling. The fear that recession could turn into deflation or even depression was far from groundless.

Yet in the medium term it was already clear by 2009 that the imbalances behind the crisis – some global, others national – needed to be resolved, and that this would require something other than Keynesian stimulus. Globally, the imbalances flowing from the macroeconomic rectangle were the most fundamental problem. How could the consumer in markets such as the US learn to borrow less and save more? Conversely, how could nations with exceptionally high savings stimulate domestic demand and reduce their dependence on exports? Nationally, it also became clear that there were imbalances to be cured, such as the sectoral bias in the UK towards financial services. There were too many engineers working in bank dealing rooms. A more stable, less geared financial market was needed in order to redress the balance.

Above all, it was certain that there would be no quick fixes: the problems of 2009 were complex and would require debate, reflection and attention to history.

Books with the benefit of a longer perspective on events will be written about the crisis unleashed in 2007. But it is safe to say this will not be the last financial crisis, for all its severity. From Edward III onward – who in 1339 repudiated his debt to his Italian creditors, thus bringing about the collapse of several Italian banks and causing widespread misery in Florence – the history of world finance could be told as a constant succession of crises.

The shorthand labels that past bubbles acquired suggest a colourful roller coaster of humanity's hope and disappointment: the tulip mania of 1637, the South Sea bubble of 1720, the Florida speculative-building bubble of 1926, the Nifty Fifty of the late 1960s, the Poseidon bubble of 1970, the dot-com bubble of 1998. They remain hard to analyse, because collective psychology plays such a vital role: financial bubbles are never just about the mathematics of economics. Bubbles can happen even when many, or even most, participants in the market are fully aware of the correct price of assets. Their dynamics are complex, and they will always be with us.

Financial crises are often linked to excessive optimism about new technology. The dot-com bubble is a prime example of this –

an equity market driven up to absurd levels on the basis of wildly optimistic estimates of the revenue generating capabilities of internet applications. But this is only the most recent case. In a very different era, the US railroad crisis of 1873 was essentially the same story. The US panic of 1873 was one of a succession of paroxysms that seized the US economy in the nineteenth century. It was sparked by the collapse of the Philadelphia banking firm Jay Cooke & Company. Cooke and other entrepreneurs had planned to build the Northern Pacific Railway – the second transcontinental railway in the US. Jay Cooke & Company provided the financing, and work was begun near Duluth in Minnesota in high optimism in February 1870. But credit rumours began to circulate about the firm, and in September 1873 it failed to market several million dollars worth of bonds in the railway. It was the final straw that led to bankruptcy. This came at a delicate moment for the US railway industry, at the tail end of a massive boom in construction, with 35,000 miles of new track laid across the country between 1866 and 1873. At the time the nation's largest employer outside of agriculture, railways involved large amounts of money and risk. Speculators caused abnormal growth and too much capital was invested in projects offering no immediate returns. The collapse of Jay Cooke triggered implosion in the industry. The New York Stock Exchange closed for ten days, and one in four of the country's more than 350 railroads went bankrupt.

The turbulence of the 1870s produced what is surely one of the greatest novels of the financial markets of all time – Anthony Trollope's *The Way We Live Now* (1875). Trollope's hero, Augustus Melmotte, arrives in London to make his mark. The cornerstone of his strategy for commercial and social success is the flotation of a project to build a railroad from the US to Mexico. It is never seriously expected to make money: the creation of an appetite for the stock is all that matters. Melmotte lives and entertains lavishly, and is lavishly generous to socially valued charities, as his paper wealth expands.

In the end, he is found out. His scheme collapses as fraud is un-covered, he is disgraced, and he commits suicide. He stands for a long line of figures down to the present day who have manipulated the markets, beguiled society, defrauded investors – and all in a desperate search (at least in his and many such cases) for recognition, for admiration, for acceptance. His story ends in tragedy, as they often do, and it is a tragedy which has replayed itself again and again in the nineteenth, twentieth and twenty-first centuries. The Greeks gave his sin a name: hubris.

Nations, too, have regularly defaulted, following the path that Edward III marked out. In the late 1990s Russia was facing a comprehensive macroeconomic collapse, involving its exchange rate, the banking system and public debt. An international rescue plan was put together and launched with an immediate liquidity injection of $22.6 billion. Russia, it was believed, was 'too big to fail', and support was essential. However, fail it did. By the summer of 1998 there were billions of dollars in unpaid wages owed to Russian workers, and monthly interest payments on Russia's debt were significantly greater than its monthly tax collections. On 17 August 1998 the government announced an immediate devaluation, with a forced restructuring of rouble-denominated public debt. This was one of two big defaults in recent times (the other being that of Argentina in 2001). But there were numerous others: an average of one a year since 1970.

A particularly problematic form of bubble that is very basic to the human psyche is the property bubble. The deep link between home and a sense of security, combined with a real fear that if you don't get on to the property ladder in time, you never will, has frequently driven people in many countries to the limits of their spending ability in inflating property prices. Housing-price crashes are particularly painful and damaging to national economies, because of the disproportionate effect on consumer confidence and the 'close-to-home' effect on behaviour. The crash of the Japanese bubble in real estate and stock prices in 1990 traumatized Japanese society for well over a decade. The experience was sufficiently scaring for President Obama to use it as a warning to those who opposed his financial stimulus package for the US economy in 2009.

Those who ignore history, it is said, are condemned to repeat it. And, on the face of it, we do learn. For example, Walter Bagehot's proposal of a new role for the Bank of England as lender of last resort, after the failure of the major London bank Overend, Gurney & Company in 1866, was first implemented in the Barings crisis of 1890. The US Federal Reserve's failure to prevent a series of domino collapses in the US banking industry in the wake of the Wall Street crash of October 1929 was not forgotten by leaders in more recent times. Globalization may be at root a phenomenon of the human spirit, but it also has very specific practical consequences – and nowhere more so than in the financial markets. The world is recognizing more and more clearly that in the financial markets everything is connected. All sorts of institutions, large and not so large, can be too interconnected to be allowed simply to fail. The lesson was to be painfully relearned in the wake of the bankruptcy of Lehman Brothers, whose effects were felt all the way from Wall Street to Hong Kong and Singapore.

Alphonse Karr (editor of *Le Figaro* from 1839 to 1848) is chiefly remembered today for coining the phrase 'plus ça change, plus c'est la même chose.' He had lived through Waterloo and the revolution of 1848 by the time he wrote it, so he had certainly seen his share of change. His phrase is now one of the most widely used French phrases in English, and at one level is true for financial crises. The historical pattern repeats and repeats. Confidence is followed by foolhardiness, then by fear followed by a crash, followed by witch-hunts – and eventually by renewed growth. The human emotions appear to repeat themselves: the greed, the panic, the shame and anger, remorse and sobriety – until exuberance reasserts itself.

And yet Mark Twain too was right: 'The past does not repeat itself, but it rhymes.' There was much that was old about the events that began to unfold in 2007, but there was also much that was new. There were defining differences: the internet, securitization, just-in-time order management, global supply chains. All these – if not completely new – had achieved a degree of intensity which meant that this was the first crisis of the global bazaar. This was a very globalized bubble, and a very globalized crisis. History moves in a spiral, not in a circle.

Thus, Alphonse Karr's world-weariness should not blind us to the fact that the world, once it recovers, will never be quite the same again. It is said of King Solomon that he had a servant whisper to him repeatedly – when things went well and when things went badly – 'This too will pass.' Crises do pass – even very intense ones. But there will be no return to the status quo ante. For the world has looked into an abyss. The experience of the 1930s led to the process of building a new world order which began at Bretton Woods in July 1944, even before the end of the Second World War. It was there that the International Monetary Fund and the International Bank for Reconstruction and Development were launched. There was to be a new world financial order for the post-war period.

After 2007–9, the manifest failure of market fundamentalism and the need for a re-balancing of the world's economy will inevitably be the starting point for a new new world order, which will profoundly change international relationships. There may be some hard-core faithful who continue to believe that business as usual will be resumed, but the consensus is that – as the former Fed chairman and market fundamentalist Alan Greenspan has acknowledged – there was to say the least a 'flaw' in the model. Society the world over demands remorse from the practitioners and action from the politicians.

In a 2009 article in the *Financial Times*, a professor of history and director of International Security Studies at Yale University, Paul Kennedy, imagined four towering economic intellects considering the crisis that began in 2007. Adam Smith, virtual founder of capitalist philosophy, would be appalled at the immorality of much consumer lending; Karl Marx, the great intellectual foe of capitalism, would get some frisson of *Schadenfreude* from the foundering of the markets; Joseph Schumpeter, popularizer of the term 'creative destruction', pro-capitalist but alert to the inherent volatility of its cycles, would broadly endorse 'our new post-excess neo-capitalist political economy ... where the animal spirits of the market will be closely watched (and tamed) by a variety of national and international zookeepers – a taming of which the great bulk of the spectators will heartily approve', as would Maynard Keynes.

Exactly how this taming will be done remains to be seen. There are many lessons to be learned from a crisis which has shocked and frightened the world – lessons for banks, and for governments and regulators, rating agencies, investors and borrowers. Banks – many of them – became overgeared and too dependent on wholesale funding (rather than real deposits from customers), as well as too focused on short-term profits at the expense of the creation of real long-term value. Regulators did not pay enough attention to liquidity management in banks, and so were not prepared for the storm when it broke. Rating agencies were too ready to work with financial engineers in the banks to help them create investment vehicles with apparently high credit quality which, as it turned out, did not stand the test of illiquidity. Investors chased yield and profit growth and forgot the 'too good to be true' test. And borrowers too often succumbed to the temptations of jam today which were proffered too freely by lenders.

In the public mind, banks have been at the epicentre of a storm of rage. The public standing of bankers is now at one of its lowest levels for decades. The sins of arrogance, greed, untrustworthiness and callousness are hard to forgive. The perception that some have taken pay and bonuses in vast multiples of the remuneration of ordinary, hard-working and socially valuable people – for indulging in an alchemy which has then blown up in their faces and required huge bailouts at prodigious cost to the taxpayer – has ignited fury around the world. And then, as economies turn down, businesses fail and unemployment rises, banks – including those that have been rescued by those same bailouts – are seem to be tugging the rug from under people's livelihoods, causing pain and further anger. Even if the truth if more complex than the headlines, re-establishing confidence in and respect for the banks will be a journey up a steep mountain.

What, then, should it look like, this new new world order? There is much that is outside the scope of this book, and many books are being or will be written on the subject. But it is clear that, whatever the eventual shape of things to come, there are four key realities that will have to be taken into account.

First, there is no alternative to the market. At its worst the market is unjust, abusive, destructive and crisis-prone, as we are all now painfully aware. Yet at its best it is a highly efficient allocator of capital, and it has delivered huge advantages to humanity. The role of capitalism in creating wealth is evident in the way it has revolutionized the Chinese, Indian and other Asian economies after they introduced market-based reforms. Even if the financial crisis leads to the first fall in world GDP since the Second World War, the last two decades of globalized market capitalism have seen extraordinary gains for hundreds of millions in previously poor societies. Churchill's famous defence of democracy – 'the worst form of government, except for all those other forms that have been tried from time to time' – applies equally well to the market. It is the worst engine of economic and social development, except for all those others that have been tried from time to time.

Second, we cannot turn the clock back either for a short time or for a longer one. We cannot go back to the 1970s, to the time before globalized capital markets: the genie is out of the bottle now, and the sorts of control that were then in place even in developed countries like the UK would no longer be considered compatible with an open society. Nor can we go back further to some 'golden age' of simpler, more communitarian, less connected living: this is completely unrealistic in what is now a densely populated, urbanized, communicating world. There is no alternative to progress and reform. China, for example, is perhaps halfway through its own internal reform process. It has a rapidly growing economy in which the private sector probably accounts for about half the total output, and banks have been comprehensively restructured and reformed. But there is a long way to go, and one of the economy's major challenges lies in the fact that the domestic capital market is as yet embryonic. There is no evidence that a modern, increasingly complex and sophisticated economy can rely on banks alone to finance development. Sustained economic progress based on more efficient capital allocation requires the development of a capital market. China will certainly want to ensure that it learns from the debacle in the international markets; but the country will equally certainly not conclude that it can afford to do without a capital market. And what is true of China is true for all economies, developed or developing. The lessons need to be learned – to restrain the excesses, to ensure transparency, to align incentives – to make the markets work better, in short, not to dismantle them.

Third, therefore, government oversight, regulation and, in times of stress, intervention are essential. Markets cannot be relied on to be stable and self-regulating. Nor are they sufficient for a balanced social development (there is no evidence that societies can rely primarily on the market for the provision of such key elements of human welfare as medical care and education). The Washington Consensus will not survive this global experience. The underlying question will be whether world leaders can construct a shared vision of a global economic order that preserves the dynamism of market forces while taming their excesses (in both risk-taking and reward). It was clear by 2009 that enhanced government cooperation internationally would be needed to facilitate effective cross-border supervision of the markets. International frameworks would be needed to deal with markets which have become irreversibly porous and interconnected. A new global order will have to build stronger institutions for international partnership.

And key to this, finally, will be an acceptance that the global balance of economic power is shifting as the centre of gravity moves from West to East. The world is being rebalanced, and it has become increasingly broadly accepted that the framework of international institutions needs to be redrawn to reflect the new realities of globalization. The developed world is going to have to make space for the newly powerful emerging economies. It is impossible to ask Asian societies to play a part in rescuing the world's financial system from collapse – to provide funds for the IMF, for example – without expecting to cede voting power to them in recognition of their new-found strength. And it is not at all surprising that they should begin to air views on the need to move away from the US dollar as the reserve currency of the world (as China has done). Such voices are going to become more and more insistent in the years to come.

The new order which will emerge – whatever its precise contours – will have to respond to these four imperatives if it is to endure. This is what is in effect recognized in the memorable statement issued in April 2009 by the London G20 summit meeting:

We start from the belief that prosperity is indivisible; that growth, to be sustained, has to be shared; and that our global plan for recovery must have at its heart the needs and jobs of hard-working families, not just in developed countries but in emerging markets and the poorest countries of the world too; and must reflect the interests, not just of today's population, but of future generations too. We believe that the only sure foundation for sustainable globalization and rising prosperity for all is an open world economy based on market principles, effective regulation, and strong global institutions.

It is worth pausing on that last sentence. After all the turmoil, despite much public resentment of and fear of globalization in many countries around the world, the leaders of countries as politically diverse as the United States of America, the People's Republic of China, the Russian Federation and the Kingdom of Saudi Arabia – to name but four out of the twenty – proclaimed that prosperity for all depends on 'an open world economy based on market principles, effective regulation, and strong global institutions'.

Amen – so be it – to that. And indeed one of the most striking manifestations of the emerging new order is precisely the role of the G20 as an increasingly central coordinating forum for the international policy response – together with the marginalization of the G7. Time will tell exactly how this forum evolves; but what is already clear is that the world has moved on irrevocably from the times when emerging markets were either uninvited or present only as a chorus. What is also striking is the degree of consensus that has been forged in the heat of the first crisis of globalization. It is inevitably easy to point to areas of vague compromise, to the risks of gaps between rhetoric and action (perhaps particularly on protectionism), to the fences not yet taken. But the contrast between international achievement in 2008–9 and the tragically short-sighted failures of 1929–32 will strike the historians of the future forcefully.

The whole tenor of the G20 statement points to the inevitable ambiguity of the markets. They are what they are because human beings are what they are: imperfect commercial animals. If ever there was an area of human activity that exemplifies the first of the three ambiguities from Chapter 1, this is it. Nigel Lawson, a former British Chancellor of the Exchequer, put it succinctly in an article in 2009: 'That capitalism has been shown, in practice, to be endemically flawed should come as no surprise. That is the nature of mankind.' But then he added this: 'What is more important is that history, notably the history of the world after the Second World War, has demonstrated beyond dispute that every other system of economic organization is far worse' – note the Churchillian defence here – 'so capitalism both deserves to survive, and will survive, just as it did after the even greater economic disaster of the 1930s.' The question is, Exactly what kind of capitalism?

We must ease our way forward. The new form of capitalism for our interconnected, globalized, complex and increasingly self-conscious world – the world that Teilhard de Chardin uncannily foresaw – will emerge slowly from the last one, but equipped with new tools and subject to new restraints. There will be no sweeping pendulum-swing from free-market fundamentalism back towards some form of centrally planned economy, or to some simpler, unconnected, pre-urban world.

The debate on the outlines of a new capitalism – more tempered and more sober – is now under way. Some have pointed to an opportunity for a 'European moment' in which relatively unfettered 'Anglo-Saxon' capitalism turns more towards a Continental-style harnessing of free markets, in the context of tighter rules and the provision of generous welfare systems. Even supporters of the Anglo-Saxon model have argued that the values of capitalism need to be reassessed: shareholder-value creation should not – as it has become in the last twenty years or so – be the be-all and end-all, the over-arching objective of management in business. It should, rather, be the result, the hallmark, of business well done. And business well done means the profitable provision of good-value services to customers.

Amartya Sen, whom we have discussed earlier, has recently

questioned the standard perception of capitalism as market-driven, profit-motivated and ownership-based, noting that all the affluent countries in the world – those in Europe, as well as the US, Canada, Japan, Singapore, South Korea, Taiwan, Australia and others – have depended for decades on transactions that occur largely outside the markets, such as unemployment benefits, public pensions and other features of social security, and the public provision of education and health care. For all their differences, these countries have in common a socio-economic approach which does not and cannot rely solely on the market.

And many people – including, for example, the premier of China, Wen Jiabao – have argued that the new capitalism should be nourished by a vision (which owes much to Adam Smith's *Theory of Moral Sentiments*) in which overspeculation is subdued by controls, and in which values other than profit (such as mutual trust and confidence) are recognized for their true worth and for their crucial role in socio-economic well-being.

It is clear, in short, that capitalism for the twenty-first century needs to rediscover a fundamentally renewed morality to underpin it. It needs to start with a question: What is progress? Is it the accumulation of wealth, or should it involve a broader definition of the quality of life which takes into account a more integrated under-standing of well-being? Surveys consistently show that economic progress has not been accompanied by the expected improved level of happiness, and that the price paid for it by many has been in the quality of human relationships. On average, people do not think of themselves as happier or better off than their parents were – even though their material standard of living is, in so many societies, unquestionably higher. And there has in particular been a marked decline in the sense of trust. The collapse in perceived trustworthi-ness is obvious with respect to the banking sector, but also applies to business more broadly – as well as in family life and in social relationships generally.

So it is not surprising that, in the public mind, free markets are under suspicion. The capitalist system is at its heart about trust. (Nowhere is this more true than in banking. The word 'credit' derives from the Latin word *credere*, meaning 'to believe'. So a credit crisis is, by the very meaning of the word, a crisis of confidence.)

If we are to restore trust and confidence in the markets, we must therefore address what is at its root a moral question. Trust and confidence cannot be restored overnight, and they cannot be restored by fiat: the process of renewal has to begin with a recognition of the moral dimension of what has happened. It is as if we have grown increasingly to accept the idea that the value of what we do is fully delineated by the market, by regulatory compliance and the law of contract. If the market will bear it, if the law allows it, if there is a contract, then no other test of rightness need apply. Yet we would not (or should not, at least) live our private lives this way. So why should it be acceptable in business?

What has happened is that we have succumbed to the sin of compartmentalization (see Chapter 1). The truth is that the value of our business is dependent on the values with which we do our business. Capitalism needs to integrate values with value. We have to recognize – boards, managements and owners alike – that values go beyond 'what you can get away with', and that values are in the end critical to value – to sustainable value, that is. Better risk management, enhanced regulation, codification of directors' responsibilities in company law – all these things are necessary. But they are not, and cannot be, sufficient without a culture of values. As individuals, we do not govern our behaviour simply by what is allowed by law or regulation. We have our own codes of conduct, and hold ourselves accountable. We take responsibility for our actions. The institutions of capitalism – businesses, banks and other institutions of the financial markets – have to do the same. This is the *sine qua non* for the restoration of public trust in the market, and is therefore essential for the overall health of society.

For companies, where does this responsibility begin? With their boards, of course. There is no other task they have which is more important. It is their job – and one which by its nature will never be complete – to promote and nurture a culture of ethical and purposeful business throughout the organization. This is true not only for banks at a time of extraordinary crisis and massive failure of public trust in the financial system, but for all businesses at all times. And the good news is that the vast, vast majority of those who work in these organizations want this. They want to be able to look at themselves in the mirror and feel confident that they and their business are making a contribution. The raw material for an ethical capitalism is present in abundance in real life. So boards and managements that take this challenge seriously will find themselves pushing on an open door.

But this soul-searching over the culture of capitalism as the world's engine of growth will not of itself let us rest easy, for other questions remain to gnaw at our conscience. What of the marginalized of the world – those who have never benefited from the burst of economic development we have seen in the last generation? And how are we going collectively to face the challenge of climate change? Aren't we just fretting about the means – the capitalist system – when we should be fretting about the end: economic development, in its present carbon-intensive form, with the grave threat it poses for the whole planet?

These are questions for the next chapter.

6

Why Should I Do Anything
for Posterity?

The new world order will be shaped by the underlying question: What is progress? Is it material wealth, or is it something more fundamental: the increased ability to create such goods as happiness, love and friendship (though we should not underestimate the part material wealth has in that)? But even if we think we have answered that question to our own satisfaction, there is another, more personal, question that looms: Why should I care? If I am as contented as can be expected and my world is well tended and well protected, why should I lift a finger?

And if I do decide to do some good, why should I do anything for anyone beyond my immediate circle? Who is my neighbour? Enlightened self-interest is based on the idea that I do good to others in order that they will do good to me. So I have no apparent reason to do good to those who are incapable of returning the favour. According to such a 'contractual' view of ethics, ethical behaviour extends only to the boundaries of our extended community, since anyone who is beyond those boundaries is hardly likely to be able to reciprocate our good deeds. Most clearly of all, this view weakens our sense of obligation to do anything for posterity, since there is no way in which those who will be alive after we are dead can do anything to make our lives better or worse now.

And yet it is impossible to escape the fact that we fret about this. We fret not just about the volatility of the world, the waywardness of the markets, and the constant disruptions of the capitalist system. We increasingly fret about ourselves, the moral implications of the way we live and what it is doing to us: to our immediate communities – the cities, towns and villages where we live – and to us as individuals – as mothers, fathers, sisters, brothers, colleagues and partners. And also to the planet as a whole.

At the core of our discomfort is the commercialization of everything. One of the immediate reactions widely triggered by the financial crisis that began in 2007 was a groundswell of rage against conspicuous consumption. The 1980s view – when you've got it, flaunt it (as the Mel Brooks song goes) – sounded hopelessly out of touch by the end of 2007, and by mid-2009 it would have been dangerous to defend it in a public place. The discovery in late 2006 that in modern Britain 70 per cent of three-year-olds recognize the McDonald's symbol but only half of them know their own surname, or that the average ten-year-old is familiar with between 300 and 400 consumer brands but would be unable to name 15 wild birds, was poignant evidence for our fears. What sort of people were we becoming?

Our fear is that the individual has been effectively replaced by the consumer. In our nightmares we are dazed and bewitched shopaholics, wandering from one glittering promise to another, overweight and weighted down with useless stuff, clutching a pack of store cards and credit cards that we can't afford. It is as if the dominant image of our time has become the shopping mall – each new one bigger, brighter, better than the last – with its myriad shopfronts, special offers, canned music and permanent artificial light.

And nothing seems sacred. The tendrils of consumerism have

wormed their way into every corner of our lives, from (long ago) Christmas, to the pylon-sprouting, ski-worn mountains, to the wedding packages on the beach or even in the supermarket aisle, to the parental rituals of children's birthday entertainers and goody bags, to the lovers' rites of Valentine's Day, to the telesales call on a Saturday morning, and to the language we use – where a relationship becomes a 'deal', an academic idea must be 'sold', and even crime is 'business'.

Whether consciously or unconsciously, we worry about where this is leading. Since Oscar Wilde's Lord Darlington, in *Lady Winder-mere's Fan*, pronounced that a cynic knows 'the price of everything and the value of nothing', it seems that we have all become cynics. If everything is defined by price, not value, then surely social fragmentation follows, since all that matters is a supply of cash rather than shared blood, community, friendship or beliefs. Yet we all know in our innermost being that price is not a reliable indicator of value. The words we use are a telling reminder of the point: what has no value is valueless; what has immense value is priceless.

As communitarian networks retreat and commercialization moves in to takes their place, we are aware, at some level, of the harsher implications. With increased efficiencies, clearer targets and the commercial pressure to do more with less come the inevitable corollaries: the risk of the waning influence of hard-to-price factors such as professional ethics, dedication beyond the call of duty, and the kindness of strangers; and the often unspoken thought that 'it's nothing to do with me.'

The effects are complex, and we should be beware of oversimplifying. At its best, the retreat of social ties and pressures has helped to increase tolerance. From the trivial level of what we wear and the gradual relaxing of class-related exclusions from clubs and paddocks, to the deeper level of removing racial and sexual barriers to the prize positions of power and influence, the individualization of the world has opened up benefits to millions who were previously shut out. At its worst, however, it has introduced a dangerous compartmentalization: the ability to walk by on the other side has rarely been greater, as we gingerly avoid involvement in other people's battles or sufferings. How, in this individualized world, can we preserve a sense of obligation? What do we teach our children? It is significant that the idea of duty seems to be coming back into public discourse, as something we yearn to retrieve from an earlier stage of history – albeit without the perceived trappings of patronization, hypocrisy and intrusiveness.

What heavy irony, too, lies in the fact that, in the most connected and networked age by far in the history of humanity, we also have fewer permanent ties and bonds to each other. Communities in every old sense have faded, and in their place have come new and fluid 'social networks' populated by restless shoals of seekers brought together by algorithms communicated through server farms in California. Is this the Teilhard de Chardin paradox in action: that only when we are One are we one – or, in other words, that only when we are fully converged with each other do we become complete persons? Is it Simmel's world: the world in which the urban metropolis drives us to objectify and put a price on everything, and in which the only route to psychological survival is to specialize and take our solitary place in an increasingly fragmented and pattern-less world, like so many misshapen pieces from a giant jigsaw puzzle without a picture on the lid?

Perhaps both the urgency of the question 'Why should I bother?' and the sharpness of the fear over isolation, privatization and fragmentation would be in some way soothed if it seemed that access to progress and self-improvement was more equitable; if it seemed that anyone, regardless of birth or background, could have a chance of participating in the fruits of the marketplace. Then, at least, it would be possible to believe that the injustices of the last generation might truly be cancelled out in the next, and that the parents who had spent a life trapped in poverty might realistically expect their children to enjoy a life of choices and comfort.

But the fact is that whole swathes of people down the ages have been denied not just equal but any kind of reasonable opportunity. Karl Marx was right to pillory the society of his time for the way in which it denied the working classes the fruits of their labour, even though he was wrong in predicting the increasing antagonism of capitalists and workers and had no inkling of the possibility of the modern welfare state or – more generally – of a capitalism which would end by making the large majority of the population think of itself as middle class.

But this has been the outcome, so far, for only a relatively privileged minority at the global level – the majority of whom live in developed countries. And while formidable progress has been made in recent decades in many developing economies too, it is clear to all that the prospects for vast numbers of human beings remain bleak.

There are many, too, who are left behind in even the wealthiest societies. One of the most important writers on the subject, the American author Ken Auletta, first popularized the idea of a section of American society that had dropped out of the normal social structure in his 1982 book *The Underclass*. By his account, this was a group not merely defined by poverty, but belonging largely to four categories: the passive poor (long-term welfare recipients), the hostile street criminals (drop-outs, drug addicts), the hustlers (dependent on the underground economy) and the traumatized (drunks, drifters, the homeless, released mental patients). By its broadest definition, the American underclass has been reckoned to comprise 36 million people at around the turn of the millennium.

In many of the modern cities of the rich West there are areas that are effectively ghettos of the marginalized, sometimes separated from the wealthiest by the shortest of distances. In London, the borough of Tower Hamlets, close by the wealthy, cosmopolitan City, is home to a 65,000-strong Bangladeshi community, the largest such group outside Bangladesh. Much of the population comes from Sylhet – a rural area of northern Bangladesh – and speaks Sylheti, a dialect with no written form. In Paris there is the notorious problem of the *banlieues*, with their heavy concentrations of North African immigrants, accompanying poverty, and regular outbursts of violent protest. Parallels have been widely drawn between colonial apartheid in Algeria, in which native medinas were kept isolated from the European neighbourhoods, and an urban profile that keeps residents of the *banlieues* trapped at a perpetual distance from the bourgeois centres of wealth and opportunity. They may be overstating the case, but all accept that there is a serious problem.

There are the marginalized in poor countries too, where the rapid improvements in overall living standards have left large sections of humanity behind. China has been a remarkable success story, with continuous economic growth since 1978 during which per-capita incomes have more than tripled and the number of extremely poor people has decreased significantly. However, it is widely recognized that living standards in rural areas in central and western China remain extremely low. Income difficulties have widened sharply in the last two decades. India has its Dalits, traditionally the lowest castes or 'untouchables', estimated in the 2001 census to number over 160 million, or 16 per cent of the population. Discrimination is widespread: many Dalits are bonded workers, and many are striving to pay off debts incurred generations before. In 2005 there were 110,000 registered cases of murder, rape and other atrocities committed against Dalits – the true figure is commonly assumed to be massively higher, since crimes against Dalits seldom get reported or go to trial. Despite great strides forward in average incomes, Brazil is well known for the tragedy of its street children, and throughout Latin America charities estimate that there are 40 million children living on the streets, with three dying from malnutrition every minute and widespread incidence of abuse and prostitution for those who manage to stay alive.

Then there is the continuing stain of slavery. By some accounts, in 2007 there were still 27 million people globally who worked in virtual slavery (although the International Labour Organization estimates that the figure is closer to 12.3 million) – the largest number (albeit probably the smallest percentage of the total human population) that has ever been enslaved at once. One anti-slavery organization claims evidence that present-day slaves have been sold for as little as $40 in Mali as young adult male labourers. And then there are over 200 million children aged from 5 to 14 who are at work around the world, according to UNICEF. Some of them are born into bondage; others are sold by their parents or abducted. They are to be found in agriculture, industry, domestic work and the sex trade.

In some cases it is whole regions that are left behind. According to the International Monetary Fund's 2008 report on Africa, the per-capita GDP of sub-Saharan Africa, excluding Nigeria and South Africa, is $435 a year, of which 44 per cent comes from exports, mainly of natural resources. Without that income from natural resources, very little of which ever gets back to the mass of ordinary people in these countries, average per-capita GDP would be $244, or around 66 cents a day – less than one-hundredth of the figure in Britain. Poverty remains endemic throughout the continent, even though recent years have seen improved growth in many countries.

In some countries, even with the best will in the world, it is hard to see how economic development can make significant progress. Burkina Faso is a small, landlocked, mostly flat country in West Africa, covering 274,200 km². The population is around 16 million, the majority of whom are farmers of cash crops such as cotton, peanuts, sesame, rice, millet and vegetables. Life expectancy is 50, and the median age 17. Low rainfall, poor soil, lack of communications, a low literacy rate, and a stagnant economy are all long-standing problems. The Sahara is slowly advancing south; the country is regularly wracked by droughts. Unless commodity resources happen to be discovered beneath the ground, it is hard to see any reason not to try to emigrate; and many do. Poverty seems to be a fact of geography.

In other countries the problem is history. Angola, for example, ought to be as rich as Switzerland. It has some of the most fertile farming land in Africa; it has rich resources of diamonds, bauxite and petroleum; it has a beautiful coast; and it is large: 1.2 million km² – about the same size as South Africa, or twice the size of Texas. And yet decades of civil war have produced an economy and society in shambles. Life expectancy is just under 40, infant mortality is extremely high (about two in ten), and many people have lost legs and arms because of landmines. The population of 13 million is one of the poorest on the planet, and, beyond oil and mineral exports, which are tightly controlled by the government, the only livelihood is a ragged patchwork of subsistence farms.

And then, more moving and more terrible somehow than the

statistics, are the individual stories. Looking the facts in the face is never easy, but when they are statistical it is easier to be detached. There is a Tearfund video made in January 2008 entitled *Bring Childhood Back to Life* which can be found on YouTube. It tells the story of Rachel Casarvo, a 13-year-old Ugandan girl, whose parents both died of Aids in 2001, leaving her to look after six children on her own. She tells the story of her days: cooking and cleaning, getting her siblings to school, and tending them when they are sick. She talks in a matter-of-fact way. And then she says simply, 'I miss my parents.' Humanity has such a propensity for compartmentalization that, like it or not, we can separate ourselves from what is going on in another continent most of the time. But a story like Rachel's brings it home that a young girl, so like my own daughters in her humanity, is one of the human beings behind the anonymous statistics.

Yet poverty is surely not inevitable, and the problem not intractable. The modern world does have the resources and the technology to deliver reasonable living standards to everyone. If you take the latest World Bank statistics, the total GDP of the world divided by its population produces an average income per head about equivalent to the standard of living in Turkey or Russia. This calculation is certainly simplistic, but it does remind us that we could at least theoretically provide every member of humankind with a standard of living which, though not rich by any means, is well beyond poverty (and beyond the incomes of well over half the world's population, bearing in mind that actual income distribution is skewed towards the rich).

In practice can this ever happen? No. It would require a global consensus and commitment which are humanly impossible to achieve. (Why? We will come back to this question in Chapter 8.) We have to accept as a matter of practical fact that the road to poverty eradication involves creating the means to economic development, rather than relying on some idealistic grand bargain of redistribution, and that it will be a long haul. And, also as a matter of practical fact, progress in poverty eradication will have to depend primarily on the markets. Imperfect, unpredictable, often brutal in their effect, they must nevertheless remain our main hope. According to the

International Finance Corporation, recent years have seen $4 of private investment flow into developing countries for every $1 in official development assistance. Remittances from overseas workers have also become a significant source of capital for some developing countries. In the case of India, such flows amount to some 3 per cent of GDP; in the case of the Philippines they amount to as much as 12 per cent.

Foreign direct investment into developing countries has fallen sharply since the onset of the global financial crisis: as always, poorer societies bear the brunt of adjustment. But it remains probable that private direct investment will over time continue to dominate the flow of capital to these areas. Foreign investment often has a mixed impact on developing economies and societies: it needs oversight, and it needs a strong sense of corporate responsibility on the part of investor if it is to deliver sustained value. But – as with the markets in general – the Churchillian defence applies. Foreign investment has often failed to benefit developing economies, yet there is no alternative to (effectively overseen, effectively governed) foreign investment as the main source of international capital for the development of most emerging markets.

Of course the markets need to be backed up. Official aid is vital. So, too, is voluntary work. The academic Michael Tanner, senior fellow at the Cato Institute in Washington, estimated some years ago that the monetary value of unpaid voluntary work in America was $176 billion. There do not seem to be any estimates at all for Africa – we can only imagine. What is clear, though, is how much hope is given to people in the world's poorest countries by dedicated, un-corrupt organizations that do their best to make a difference with sparse resources. The British journalist Matthew Parris, in an article in *The Times* published in December 2008 about his return to Malawi after forty-five years' absence, described how the Christian charity Pump Aid not only helped people keep their village wells clean but, on a more profound level, also helped them to work with 'honesty, diligence and optimism' – by giving them back a belief in themselves.

There are also specific intervention mechanisms that are obviously effective. For instance, in 2000 at the World Economic Forum in Davos, a group including the Bill & Melinda Gates Foundation, the World Health Organization, the World Bank, UNICEF and the vaccine industry in both industrialized and developing countries launched the Global Alliance for Vaccines and Immunization – or GAVI for short. The aim is the worldwide expansion of childhood vaccination to significantly reduce childhood mortality before 2015. GAVI estimates that of the more than 10 million children who die before reaching their fifth birthday every year, 2.5 million die from diseases that could be prevented with vaccines – largely pneumococcal diseases or rotavirus (a severe form of diarrhoea). Since its launch, GAVI has vaccinated more than 200 million children and claims to have prevented over 3 million deaths. The effectiveness of well-funded, focused and collaborative action like this is plain for all to see.

One of the most remarkable development phenomena of recent decades has been the spread of microfinance. In 1974 an economics lecturer at the University of Chittagong in Bangladesh lent $27 to a group of women in the nearby village of Jobra who made bamboo furniture. They had previously had to take out usurious loans in order to buy bamboo; they then sold these items to the moneylenders to repay them, with barely any profit to show for their work. The traditional banks – predictably – were loath to make tiny loans at normal interest rates to such poor people, who were classified as high risk and deemed unlikely to be able to repay the loans. What the economics lecturer discovered was that in fact the women were very good credit risks, and that lending to them at reasonable rates enabled them to develop their small businesses on a sound basis. Thirty years later that same economics lecturer, Muhammad Yunus, won the Nobel Peace Prize, and microfinance – financial services for the very poor – had achieved a resounding record of success in reaching the excluded and assisting small groups of people to take control of their own lives. In 2006 it was estimated that there were around 90 million beneficiaries of microfinance worldwide. The majority of users are women, because they control the household funds and because they are so often responsible for the productive work done in the community. Time and time again, the experience has been of very low default rates on microfinance lending. This first step in connecting these women to a wider world through marketing what they produce is a powerful means of empowerment. It may not make people rich; nonetheless, it is profoundly transformative.

Eradicating poverty is not a fantasy. The US economist Jeffrey Sachs has summed up the problem: 'Ours is the first generation in the history of the world with the ability to eradicate extreme poverty. We have the means, the resources and the know-how. All we lack is the will.' But progress will be long drawn out, and elementary mathematics highlights the scale of the challenge. In some of the poorest countries of the world, average incomes are perhaps $200 per year. At a sustained growth rate of 10 per cent – which requires very strong economic performance by any standards – halfway through this century income per head would still be less than that of Brazil today. In other words, our grandchildren will still be struggling with development issues that will be easily recognizable to students of contemporary affairs. Corruption and civil disorder will probably still disfigure some of the most disadvantaged countries in the world. And poor people will still bear the brunt of natural disasters. The problem of world poverty will not have been solved to the satisfaction of the human conscience in the lifetime of anyone presently alive.

But if the poor will always be with us, does this make it too easy to give up, too easy to conclude that the effort is not worth the candle? Why should I do anything for posterity? This is really two separate questions. First, what good would it do anyway, what difference would it make? And, second, what has all this got to do with me?

As for the first question, there clearly are differences that can be made. We have touched on some above – the direct interventions and the less direct, all of them helping to alleviate suffering where it is most acute and create opportunity for human beings to fulfil their potential. We might think too of Tim in Kolkata with his two hundred children from the streets of the city. Even one child's life lived fully is difference enough. And the second question: What has all this got to do with me? This demands a detailed response. But, before we turn to it, what about the other great anxiety of the age of globalization – climate change and environmental degradation? Can our planet cope?

Fears about planetary exhaustion have been with us for a long time. When, in *A Christmas Carol*, Scrooge explains why he refuses to donate to the poor who will not enter a workhouse ('If they would rather die, they had better do it, and decrease the surplus population'), Dickens is putting into his mouth the ideas of Thomas Malthus, an eighteenth-century English clergyman who – in his *An Essay on the Principle of Population*, first published in 1798 – achieved huge influence in his lifetime and beyond for raising the alarm about population growth. He saw the earth's resources running out in the face of relentlessly increasing numbers of people following the Industrial Revolution, and argued against the Poor Laws and the repeal of the Corn Laws on the grounds that these were measures that would merely make matters worse by increasing the population. His fundamental assertion that population could not increase logarithmically for ever is believed to have helped Darwin form the theory of natural selection.

In 1972, Malthusian thinking lay behind an influential book entitled *The Limits to Growth*. This report, commissioned by a think tank known as the Club of Rome, set out to explore how far exponential economic and population growth could continue in a world with finite resources. It unleashed a torrent of alarm, furious argument and heated criticism – and clearly touched a public nerve. Many read into the book predictions that were not there, or perhaps were only implied by some of the formulas used by the authors: for instance, that the earth's supply of oil would run out by 1992. But the overriding thought that humanity was running out of food and fuel was a populist hit, sparking off a whole literature of predictions and proposals involving everything from mining asteroids to grey goo (a large mass of replicating nano-robots).

A common thread of these resource-centric fears has always been that the poorer populations would drag back more advanced societies because of the sheer scale of their needs. The thought behind much of the argument was, How were the rich countries going to restrain the poor countries from threatening their well-being?

Today the dominant fear about our planet is the more dramatic catastrophe that could be caused by global climate change. Resources are still finite, of course, but there is a greater readiness now to believe in the power of human inventiveness and technology to maximize resource extraction and efficiency. Global warming, on the other hand, could be the prologue to a tragedy of unimaginable scale. The world already feels like a less predictable and hospitable place as it is racked by increasing incidences of drought and flooding, fire and storm, melting and freezing. At one of Uganda's two national newspapers, the *Daily Monitor*, in 2008 it was decided that for the first time in its history the paper should carry a weather map – the reason being that, for the first time anyone could remember, the country's weather had become malignly unpredictable.

Not that everyone greets the prospect of climate change with alarm. There is special pleading in several developed countries claiming to welcome a degree of global warming. Scientists may condemn them as trivial or irresponsible, but the fact these voices exist could affect the political resolve to act at the highest level. In November 2008, for example, a group made up mainly of university economists and anthropologists released a report pitted directly against the leading publicists of global-warming disaster such as the former US vice-president Al Gore and the British conservationist James Lovelock. The group said that global warming might not be the unmitigated disaster that it was often represented to be: indeed, that for certain northerly regions such as Canada, Russia and Scandinavia it might be quite welcome. One of the group, Robert Mendelsohn, an economics professor from Yale, pointed out the benefits for Canada – from a longer growing season to the opening-up of shipping routes through the Northwest Passage. Others pointed out the benefits of tourism in previously inhospitable cold regions. Another, Benny Peiser, an anthropologist from John Moores University in Liverpool, argued that the current slow upward trend in global temperatures could prove beneficial to human health, and said that in periods of warming there tended to be 'thriving societies' with greater than normal progress in economic and social development. Meanwhile, from another angle, Patrick Michaels, of the Cato Institute, suggested that scientists have a natural interest in alarmism, since bad news leads to government action and government action usually leads to funding research, which is the key to scientists' professional advancement.

Yet the evidence is real and unavoidable. Some of it we can experience with our own senses. As we have noted in Chapter 4, pollution is now a major challenge for many emerging markets. And we should not find comfort too easily in the thought that this is a transitional problem of economies passing through the industrial phase of economic development. For one thing, pollution is not confined to big cities in emerging markets: in hot summers in Paris and Athens, cars have had to be banned from the centre at certain times to avoid the dangerous build-up of exhaust fumes. For another, it would require a heroic degree of optimism, given the sheer scale of urbanization under way over the next half-century, to believe anything other than that the volume of urban pollution is going to go on increasing even if some cities are successful in moving towards a cleaner environment.

Other evidence of damage to the planet is less likely to register with us in our daily lives and, while we may know it in the abstract, we need a jolt to bring it home. For me, such a jolt came when I saw extraordinary satellite pictures of Borneo, taken at five-yearly intervals from 1985 onward, which show clearly to the naked eye the massive reduction in forest cover. When this is represented graphically – as it is on the World Wildlife Fund's website – the map of Borneo turns from a lush green to a parched yellow between 1985 and a projected version of how it is likely to look in 2020. I have seen with my own eyes the beauty of the primeval forest of Borneo. I have seen how sustainable logging can preserve its essential character and its biodiversity. I have also seen the impact of unsustainable and destructive exploitation on an environment which is fragile, precious and effectively irreplaceable.

The picture is similar in South America. The Amazon rainforest is disappearing at an average rate of about 1 per cent a year. This means that, if it keeps up that rate, within less than fifty years it will be half gone. Again, satellite photographs graphically capture the progressive deforestation. Currently about 6.7 million km^2 of forest – about half the planet's remaining rainforest and the largest and most species-rich tract of tropical rainforest in the world – the Amazon rainforest lost over 200,000 km^2 of trees in the decade leading up 2005 in Brazil alone. In December 2008 the Brazilian government said that satellite imagery had shown deforestation accelerating again for the first time in four years, owing to illegal logging and high commodity prices.

Finally, there is all the evidence that is scientifically known and statistically measurable but which the naked eye cannot see. Notwithstanding scepticism in some quarters about the effects of global warming (in many ways an unfortunate term), there is no denying the remorseless rise of the major 'greenhouse gases' (which absorb and emit radiation) in the atmosphere. Taking the global long-term trends of the five major gases that contribute to global warming (carbon dioxide, methane, nitrous oxide, CFC-12 and CFC-11) and putting them on a graph, there is no mistaking the trend. The growth trajectory for carbon dioxide, methane and nitrous oxide is a straight line heading upward. Only the two CFCs – the gases used in refrigerators – show recent declines in their growth rates (an example of concerted action that works). Since 2000 there have been particularly sharp accelerations in global CO_2 emissions, to more than three times the level of the 1990s.

How can this trend be reversed? The arithmetic is brutal. At present, average CO_2 emissions per head are 7 tonnes per year. Just to prevent the earth's mean temperature from rising more than 2 degrees by 2050 requires that this be reduced to around 2 tonnes per year: i.e. around India's present level – but half that of China, one-sixth that of Europe, and one-tenth of North American levels.

Even more clearly than in the case of poverty, this challenge cannot be left to the market alone to meet. Until the world has an effective framework for charging those who emit CO_2 into the atmosphere, there is no economic incentive not to do so. The damage it does will not be visible for many years, and, when it is, it will not be attributable to any particular agent. All it costs is the common good. The climate, as economists say, is the quintessential 'commons', the public good that is free to everyone. When the *Stern Review,* the most comprehensive review ever carried out on the economics of climate change, was published in October 2006, the author Nicholas Stern announced at the launch that the world would have to muster 'all the economics we can bring to bear' on climate change to prevent a catastrophe. He continued, 'The science tells us that greenhouse gas emissions are an externality; in other words our emissions affect the lives of others. When people do not pay for the consequences of their actions we have market failure. This is the greatest market failure the world has seen.'

That is why government must give the market direction. And, given the right direction and the right incentives, harnessed instead of paralysed, the market can be a very powerful servant of humanity in tackling climate change. A precondition for this is human coopera-tive endeavour. The United Nations Climate Change Conference in Copenhagen at the close of 2009 is a huge potential opportunity. One of the key issues that has to be resolved is how to price the output of carbon dioxide so that markets can begin to work on restraining it. The two main pricing mechanisms proposed are (i) to charge a tax on each tonne of carbon dioxide emitted into the air and (ii) to place a cap on total emissions and then let polluters trade emission permits. As, for example, Steve Lohr of the *New York Times* has argued, economically, a cap-and-trade system has the same goal as a tax, putting a price on CO_2 emissions, but it goes about it differently. Such a system has some political advantages. The biggest polluters, who would have to invest the most to make changes, could be given allowances to start with. It can also deflect the anger over higher costs and enable governments to use their allocations to buy political support, since permits are the equivalent of cash. Precisely for this reason, some economists advocate an explicit tax as the clearest price signal to the energy marketplace, and one which is less susceptible to political tampering and manipulation than a cap-and-trade system.

Whichever route is chosen, what Eileen Claussen, president of the US Pew Center on Global Climate Change, said in her remarks on emissions reductions in 2002 remains as true as ever:

If you are a business, or an investor, the market is the environment within which you operate. And as society comes to grips with climate change, the rules of the market will change. The climate will stop being free. There will be a cost for emitting carbon. From the business perspective, that will be the most important new reality. And it will require some adjustment. Those who understand that reality, and make the adjustment, will not only survive but thrive. Because in every change there is opportunity, and the rewards flow to those who seize it first. But by the same token, those who ignore this new reality and fail to adjust will pay the price. The market is a harsh arbiter. It will figure out quickly enough who's done a good job of managing their carbon risk, and who has not. If you want to make sure you're a market winner in the carbon-constrained world of the future, and not a loser, the time to start is now.

Moreover, the sobering thought is that the technological means and resources to meet the challenge *are* available. There are numerous examples of practical initiatives which have the potential to make a difference in very local ways. One such innovation – developed by the Energy and Resources Institute of India, a uniquely influential body working at the intersection between ecological and development challenges – is the solar-powered lamp. This device, conceptually simple like so many truly valuable innovations (microfinance is another example), brings light to homes in small villages with no access to electricity, at minimal costs to the environment. 'Lighting a billion lives' is the Institute's watchword. If this vision can be realized in the coming years, it could have a profound impact on rural poverty (as microfinance has had), and at the same time deliver its benefits on a low-carbon basis.

This is just one example. The general point is that sustainable growth and the transition to a low-carbon economy *can* be achieved by common endeavour at a reasonable cost. According to a report by the McKinsey Global Institute in the summer of 2008, it is possible to conceive of action on climate change that supports two apparently contradictory objectives at the same time: stabilizing greenhouse gases *and* maintaining economic growth. Reconciling these two objectives means that 'carbon productivity' (the amount of GDP produced per unit of carbon equivalents emitted) must increase dramatically: from approximately $740 GDP per tonne of CO_2 today to $7,300 GDP per tonne of CO_2 by 2050 – a tenfold increase, comparable to the labour-productivity increases of the Industrial Revolution. However, the 'carbon revolution' must be achieved in one-third of the time that economic transformation took then, in order to maintain current growth levels while keeping CO_2 levels safe. McKinsey reckon that the macroeconomic costs of this carbon revolution are likely to be manageable, being in the order of 0.6 per cent to 1.4 per cent of global GDP by 2030. Borrowing could potentially finance many of the costs, thereby effectively limiting the impact on short-term GDP growth. In fact, depending on how new low-carbon infrastructure is financed, the transition to a low-carbon economy could increase annual GDP growth in many countries.

However, it is clear that the threat of climate change cannot be addressed in isolation from the challenge of poverty. There is no prospect of global agreement on a significant shift to low-carbon economic development that does not encompass equally significant support for poorer countries determined at all costs to raise material standards of living. There is no alternative, therefore, to a common endeavour which is comprehensive in its scope and has no historical precedent in its ambition.

Yet the history of common endeavour is only partially encouraging. Most examples of success have depended on either narrow focus or strong leadership. The eradication of smallpox was a success. It was precise and effective – as was the campaign to curb use of CFCs in the 1990s. The demonstration of strong leadership has achieved impressive results just often enough in world history to give a reasonable expectation of hope. The naval supremacy of Britain in the early nineteenth century gave it the power to move to suppress the slave trade and outlaw slavery in British colonies. The European Recovery Program, or Marshall Plan, of 1948 would never have come into being without the leadership of the US president

Harry Truman and the US Secretary of State George Marshall, whose speech at Harvard in June 1947 included the following patient vision:

It is logical that the United States should do whatever it is able to do to assist in the return of normal economic health in the world, without which there can be no political stability and no assured peace. Our policy is directed not against any country or doctrine but against hunger, poverty, desperation, and chaos. Its purpose should be the revival of a working economy in the world so as to permit the emergence of political and social conditions in which free institutions can exist.

But when leadership becomes more fractured, progress is more difficult. World trade negotiations are an example. In the post-war period, under US leadership, agreement on world trade made material progress. Latterly leadership has been more multiplex, and the project has become more complex – which is all evidenced in the painful lack of progress at the Doha round of talks. It has to be hoped that this is not an augury for international negotiations on climate change. Wherever common endeavour is needed, the parochial and the short term are real and present dangers. The serious challenge will be in settling which countries bear what share of the burden of adjustment. As one South African commentator put it, it is as if the developing countries have been invited to join the rich countries for dessert towards the end of an expensive dinner, and then asked to split the bill. Agreeing the share of the burden without watering down global targets will require at least as much political courage and leadership as was shown by Truman and Marshall in 1948.

There are clear implications in all this for agents beyond governments – for voluntary associations, businesses and individuals. Common endeavour demands a response by all and at every level. In a world where so much of the life of the human spirit has been privatized, where individualization has swept through society, we must consider how the possibility of constructive action helps to answer the question of why we should indeed consider doing something for posterity – whatever it may or may not have done for us.

*

Which brings us back to the question posed at the end of the last chapter. Is the issue really the end rather than the means? Is the real villain of the piece carbon-intensive economic development – rather than its servant, the capitalist market? Has the human species become addicted to (carbon-intensive) economic growth? And if so, how do we free ourselves from this addiction?

What is clear is, first, that the rich know – or should know – what the answer should be as soon as they face this question. They know somewhere in themselves that there are diminishing marginal returns to incremental wealth – that the second glass of wine never tastes as good as the first one, that enough is eventually enough. They can be seduced into the pursuit of rarity – antique coins, classic cars, vintage wines, fashionable art, and so on – and be persuaded to pay for them precisely because of their distinctiveness. But when confronted with the question, they know these are optional extras. Enough has become enough.

The poor of the world, needless to say, have a different perspective. 'God dares not appear to a starving man,' Gandhi once said, 'except in the guise of bread.' And, by extension, we can hardly expect the emerging world not to strive for what the developed world takes for granted – first, clean water and electricity, then air conditioning, mechanized transport and all the rest of it. Conversely, the developed world may be prepared to agree with the proposition that enough is enough, but it is not at all clear that it would agree so readily that less is enough.

Each needs the other as partner to meet the twin challenges of the reduction of material poverty through economic growth (because there is no other way) and the shift to a low-carbon economy for the benefit of our grandchildren (and beyond). We have to wrestle with the two problems together and collectively. There is no alternative, and success in time is not guaranteed. And we need all the victories we can get: hence the importance of the emerging international framework based on the G20 process; hence the importance of the Doha round; hence the importance of Copenhagen. Hence the importance of continuing these processes even when their results at any given event may be disappointing.

And the other thing to which there is no alternative is the market. The development of poorer countries needs it; the development of a low-carbon economy needs it. It is clearly neither perfect nor sufficient for either challenge; it is equally clearly indispensable. Without it, we condemn poor countries to endless marginalization, and we guarantee that the low-carbon economy will remain largely a matter of rhetoric. Working with the grain of the markets, on the other hand, humanity can harness a force which is deeply engrained in its own nature to achieve what can easily seem to be the impossible.

All this involves the denial of compartmentalization. It will demand an integrated response from all of us as members of society, as institutions and as individuals. Governments alone cannot save the planet.

Businesses – of all kinds, in the real economy or in the financial system – cannot therefore take the view that this is none of their business. As was argued in the last chapter, their challenge – made all the more pressing by the huge breakdown in public trust and confidence in recent years – is to recognize the values on which the value (i.e. long-term sustainable shareholder value) of their business depends. And, at this juncture in the history of our development, those values are inextricably linked with the question of those twin challenges and how we face them.

'Corporate social responsibility' has entered the lexicon of business in recent years, as it should. Latterly there is a trend to replace it with the term 'corporate sustainability'. Either expression is a reminder of the broad responsibility that businesses need to accept. There is of course always the danger that the words become part of the rhetoric of brand management – empty slogans which have no real impact on behaviour. There is also the subtler danger that corporate social responsibility is defined and departmentalized – or compartmentalized – into a range of activities carried out by a 'CSR function' as an adjunct to the mainstream business.

The danger lies in mistaking the activities of the CSR function (the charity sponsorships, the community action, the educational mentoring etc.) – valuable though those unquestionably can be – for facing up to the all-embracing need to accept the responsibility of building the business in a way which sustainably enhances the common good. Corporate social responsibility is not just about community support; corporate sustainability is not just about managing the company's carbon footprint. It is about the strategic objectives, and indeed the *raison d'être*, of the company itself.

Does this conflict with the job of maximizing shareholder value? Only if that is interpreted as a short-term project. But it is no part of the responsibility of a board to focus on the short term. There is no question but that the markets – that anonymous term which is in fact the sum of countless voices of investors and traders – have often pressured boards and managements in recent years to do exactly that. Some of the results of such pressure are now plain for all to see, and the breakdown in society's trust in the system has been the result.

The response has to be renewed commitment to the real task of sustainable value maximization. And it is clear that this has four elements. First, there is of course the direct and basic responsibility to earn as good a return as is sustainably possible on the capital entrusted to the company by its shareholders. No broader understanding of business responsibility can be an excuse for fuzzy and unrealistic strategic objectives, poor competitive positioning, or operational inefficiencies. And, second, it is perhaps standard textbook wisdom that, in order to earn the best return over time, businesses need to nurture their customer relationships and service. But increasingly these days this in turn requires them to demonstrate a wider commitment to the community and the environment. It is not for nothing that so many retail businesses nowadays market 'green' or 'fair-trade' products. What was once unusual – even quirky – is now commonplace, and is a response to growing consumer consciousness of wider connections. The cynic might argue that some of this is tokenism, or that it remains marginal in significance. But if the consensus on the entangled issues of poverty and climate change is right, it would be wiser to see this as a rising tide.

What is indisputable is that a third element of value maximization – the way a business engages with its people – takes us straight into the realm of sustainability and social responsibility. As argued in the last chapter, the vast majority of people want to be able to see themselves and the work they do, the business they are in, as making a contribution to society. And it is abundantly clear – as any businesses which have regular graduate recruitment programmes will know – that the next generation of management demands to know what the policies of the company are for meeting the challenge. Moreover, anyone who has seen the way in which community involvement exhilarates colleagues in the workplace cannot fail to recognize the impact this has on their engagement with their work. Nothing better illustrates the importance of a holistic approach to the well-being – and therefore effectiveness – of people at work. I recall meeting a colleague at a business processing centre in Hyderabad, India: he had recently returned from a two-week project with the charity Earthwatch on Lake Baikal in Russia, where they had helped in the work of cataloguing the extraordinary fauna and flora of the world's largest body of fresh water. His bubbling enthusiasm for all he had experienced spilled over into his workplace, and was infectious all round. The consciousness-raising value of this and the countless other ways in which people from the workplace engage with the wider world – whether close at hand or far afield – is priceless.

The fourth element of sustainable value maximization is therefore the way in which the business engages with the communities in which it operates (which may mean a very local focus in the case of a small business, or a broad global canvas in the case of large multinational corporations). If there was ever a time when this was an optional extra, that time has gone. From politicians to the media, to people in the business, to the customers and to shareholders, the expectations are increasingly clear and vocal. And this means that any business which values its brand, and understands how the brand represents – or should represent – the essence of the company's self-understanding and *raison d'être*, will see this challenge as integral to sustainable success. It means that the company has to be able to ask – and give a satisfactory answer to – the question: How does the business we do contribute to the common good?

And boards and senior managements need to be able to explain the answer convincingly to their own people. (In the case of banking, for example, how do specific financial products contribute to human welfare and economic development?) This is not just a matter for strap lines and sales manuals: it should be a central task of training and development programmes to help employees understand how their roles make this contribution. And if that begs an uncomfortable question, then it is the corporate social responsibility of the company, at board level, to face up to that question. (For the record, I believe that, while banking has had much to answer for in recent years, as discussed in the last chapter, it is an activity which is essential to sustainable economic development. Strong, efficient, well-supervised banks with a drive to innovate and to provide suitable, profitable services, and staffed by people with integrity and commitment, are a *sine qua non* of effective market economies and modern social development, the relief of poverty, and our future as a low-carbon economy.)

All these elements are mutually reinforcing. Good customer relationships and engaged people are essential to profit growth. Community commitment nurtures customer relationships and people development. Sustainable profits underpin investment in people and community. Remove any of the components and the circuit is broken. The older, simpler, Friedmanite idea that the sole job of a business is to create profit for shareholders has proved insufficient to sustain value and – in the end – a bad deal for shareholders. Sustainable profit and corporate social responsibility are not in conflict: they are interdependent.

It is in this context that companies need to approach the sensitive issue of remuneration. There has been widespread discomfort with the way the markets have widened income disparities – even if most recognize that it is hard to escape the laws of supply and demand to any great extent, and harder still in an increasingly open world where many people can move and far more jobs can move. Governments need to regulate for transparency and to eliminate distortion, as they certainly will – and should – in the financial markets in the wake of the recent experience. For it has become clear that in many cases there has been far too much focus on the short term and – to say the least – insufficient alignment with the real long-term interests of the company and its owners. But, as a matter of practical fact, the laws of supply and demand operate in the market for people as well as in the market for goods and services. And they will always produce differentials. We will return to the question of the challenges this poses for individuals later in this chapter. For now, we need to recognize that the markets are always liable to cause tension within society (as Polanyi highlighted so clearly), and the question of what is enough of a reward is not – as a matter of social reality – something which interests only the individual and the employer. Getting the balance right, so that companies have and retain the management they need to achieve sustainably profitable growth – with all that this means for the common good – is one of their most important corporate social responsibilites.

Other institutions – charities, churches, community organizations, schools, etc. – in fact any organizations that seek to have a life beyond the term of their current people – face analogous responsibilities. They too have brands, or reputations, to nurture and develop. Indeed, there are some charitable brands which are as old and well established as any corporate brand: the Red Cross carries a reputation nurtured carefully since 1863, the National Trust since 1895, Oxfam since 1942. At their best, like corporations at their best, such organizations are sustained, consciously or unconsciously, by attention to the same four basic elements of value. Any such organization which depends on donor support has a responsibility analogous to the corporate profit objective: the responsibility to deliver results that represent a 'return' on the funds – the duty to perform and be efficient. Then, secondly, the analogue to the customer relationship of the corporate world might be said to be the challenge of providing good services to those intended to benefit from the organization's activities. And, so far as people engagement and community commitment are concerned, exactly the same responsibilities apply as in the case of any commercial business. There is more in common – and perhaps increasingly more in common – between these worlds of business and of non-commercial organizations than the ideology of market fundamentalism would have wanted to acknowledge.

Finally, there is that question we left hanging earlier in this chapter: What has all this got to do with me? There is, in other words, the challenge of what might be described – in parallel to corporate social responsibility – as individual social responsibility. We have seen in the previous chapter how the market has an apparently inevitable tendency to create inequality. Often (and especially latterly) its distorted operation has created far too much inequality. Yet differentiation will always be there – only the degree of it is variable. And therefore there will always be those who have not merely more than others, but more than they could conceivably need. There are only two possible responses to this fact for those of us in this position: we can, in effect, shrug our shoulders; or we can hear the still, small voice of conscience. That voice reminds us – if we listen – that something is owed by the affluent. And a debt not paid makes a debtor who is guilty. Hence that voice. We often hear affluent people speaking of wanting to 'give something back to the community' – the very phrase conveys a sense that something is owed. At its worst, this response may be little more than a transaction à la Melmotte: doing something because it is expected, and because it wins social points. In which case it is simply one more transaction of the kind discussed by Simmel – the objectification of human relationships through the medium of money and exchange. At its heart, this is not giving back what is owed: rather, it is a transaction which is an investment.

At its best, though, a different – and deeper – form of transaction takes place when we respond to that voice. The giver discovers that his or her spirit becomes involved, and may then even experience an inkling of a sense that the debt is not just being repaid in the giving, but being forgiven. And the sense that the debt is forgiven in the giving can then bloom into a sense that the debtor is forgiven – for all the imperfections through which the affluence has been generated, and for all the presumption that the affluence may have generated in its time.

How far do we take this? What are the specific obligations to the wider world of those who are in the top half of the scale of world income? Of those whose carbon footprint is well above the world average? Of those, in particular, who occupy senior positions and leadership roles in well-paid industries? Of anyone who, from a global perspective, counts as wealthy?

The answers certainly include extensive giving – and the ancient biblical principle of tithing (i.e. donating 10 per cent of earnings) is surely not nearly enough in the case of the affluent who earn more – and often far more – than needed for any definition of a reasonably comfortable life. 'What is enough?' is a question that demands an individual, personal response. But the litmus test is surely whether it is both real and significant and feels like a costly personal commitment in response to the challenge.

No less important is the question of talent and time. And, in the context of the frenetic lives of the modern affluent, it is perhaps time above all which is the real scarce resource, and the giving of time which is the bigger sacrifice. For that reason – because of its importance to the wholeness of the human being – it is perhaps subjectively even more important than the money donated.

Which reminds us that, like its corporate parallel, individual social responsibility cannot be an optional extra or an adjunct to a life focused purely on work (or pleasure). The response thus goes well beyond the giving of time, talent and money. The responsibility involves the whole person: it cannot be limited by compartmentalization, or discharged just by writing cheques. And the more the whole person is involved, the more we will discover an old truth about giving and receiving, and about redemption and renewal. To borrow and adapt words associated with a figure from medieval times who can seem impossibly remote from our modern life experience – St Francis of Assisi – we will discover that it is in giving that we are forgiven, and in forgiving that we receive.

And if we do not discover this, we risk discovering something else about ourselves – as we shall see in the next chapter.

7

Faust and the Rich Young Man

But stay awhile – O, how beautiful you are!
                    Goethe, *Faust* (completed 1832)

Take all your treasure, sell it, give it to the poor; and come,
follow me, for you will have treasure in heaven.
                    St Mark's Gospel

Either we discover the old truth about commitment which we explained at the end of the last chapter – about giving and receiving, about sacrifice – or we discover another truth: that we cannot fulfil ourselves in the global marketplace.

Time and again we experience the truth of the old clichés.

We learn, for instance, that ambition for power can deceive. The (perhaps apocryphal) deathbed sayings of the powerful tell a story which resonates well beyond the particular legacies of the people concerned. William the Conqueror – he who triumphed, on the only date in history that all Britons can remember, at the Battle of Hastings, thus inaugurating a reign which lasted twenty-one years and began the radical transformation of England from Saxon communitarianism to Norman feudalism – is alleged to have shown uncharacteristic remorse at the end of it all: 'I've persecuted the natives of England beyond all reason, whether gentle or simple. I have cruelly oppressed them and unjustly disinherited them, killed innumerable multitudes by famine or the sword and become the barbarous murderer of many thousands both young and old of that fine race of people.'

Or there is Cardinal Wolsey, the great prince of the Church and servant of Henry VIII. In disgrace with his king because of his failure to procure the annulment of Henry's marriage to Catherine of Aragon, he died on his way from York to London and probable execution in 1530. 'Had I but served my God as I have served my king, I should now be a happy man' he is alleged to have uttered – the words of a man who has given too much to his career; words which stand for the disappointment of those who lose power in a thousand different circumstances: politicians at the hands of electorates; company chief executives at the hands of boards under pressure from dissatisfied shareholders; those who hitch their wagons to the stars of ruthless tyrants only to be dropped by them when they cease to be useful.

We also know of the driven man who relentlessly pursues whatever goals he sets for himself at the expense of any real relationships with other human beings, often crushing those nearest him in the process, and without finding any peace for himself. *Citizen Kane*, Orson Welles's film masterpiece, made in 1941 when he was only 25, is widely accepted to be based on the life story of William Randolph Hearst. It is a fictional account of a newspaper magnate who enjoys all the visible trappings of success, yet whose dark secret is a lonely, unspoken, perhaps not ever acknowledged yearning for his childhood innocence – symbolized dramatically by the toboggan he played with as a child, named 'Rosebud'. He dies with the word 'Rosebud' on his lips – to the puzzlement of those around his bed. And they miss the only clue to what it refers to or what it means. The final seconds of the film reveal a man for whom driving ambition was never more than compensation for a child's longing for home.

For the majority of people, of course, the clichés are more mundane. They don't find themselves at 'the top of the greasy pole' – to use Disraeli's vivid image – and are more at risk from the workaholism or the shopaholism of the global bazaar than from the drive to dominate.

Workaholism is an occupational hazard of recent times. As the Industrial Revolution gathered momentum in the nineteenth century, men, women and children were put to work too young and for too long. Gradually, legislation began to bring humanity to the workplace, and from the late nineteenth century onward trade unions began to offer more and more effective protection. With the rise of the welfare state, of a service economy and of broad-based prosperity, the days of industrial oppression are largely gone in the wealthy countries of the G7. But they have been replaced, for many, by an unremitting market capitalism which has made more people feel middle class – but which has also required the middle class to work harder than ever. 'I feel I have missed my children growing up' – the lament is heard time and again in the feverish market places of London, New York, Frankfurt and elsewhere. Technology should have made work easier. It has done the reverse: the email and the Blackberry presumptuously demand immediate responses on an almost literally round-the-clock, global basis.

And then there is the money – either for what it can buy or just for itself. At one level, as Simmel understood, a leveller and a liberator; at another, a seductive addiction about which all the clichés are true. As the sayings go, you cannot take it with you, it doesn't make you happy, and you can only eat three meals a day. The legends which tell the story again and again go back a long way: King Midas of Phrygia asks the gods to turn anything he touches to gold. They grant him his wish. Everything he touches turns to cold metal. Be careful what you wish for, lest you get it.

We cannot fulfil ourselves in business through power or work or wealth. We learn this in a variety of ways. Events can turn on us: we get passed over for the promotion we covet so much – or we get it and find that we drink from a poisoned chalice. Or tragedy strikes: illness or untimely death in the family, which suddenly reminds us of the transience of it all and of what we have laid on the altar of sacrifice. Or we wake in the middle of the night – that time when all human experience knows that the spirits are at their lowest – and take stock, perhaps, and realize that the clock is ticking. One way or another, we struggle to possess, and fear we have ended by being possessed – or rejected. Is there anyone, successful or un-successful by their own lights or in the eyes of the world, who has not sensed this in some way at some time?

It is one of the oldest stories of all. And one of its most powerful embodiments is in the legend of Faust, the man who makes a bargain with the Devil. In one guise or another, the Faust story recurs time and again in European literature. Its enduring fascination into the present age rests precisely on the fact that it is so telling about the besetting sin of the human spirit in the global bazaar.

The original Faust was probably a showman, astrologer and alchemist. He was born around 1480, in Knittlingen, north of Pforzheim in Germany. He was notorious even during his lifetime, being accused of all kinds of misdemeanours – some believable, others plainly mythical. But above all he has gone down in legend as the man who made a pact with the Devil, selling his soul in return for all the pleasures of the world.

In sixteenth- and seventeenth-century Protestant Germany, Faust was the subject of long sermonizing tracts. He also became a regular subject for popular theatre and puppet performances, presented with plenty of burlesque and colour. He played perfectly to an enduring human fascination with mischief: Faust's end, in the flames of hell, was the ideal combination of spine-chilling excitement and morality tale for the masses.

But the story became more than that, thanks largely to two works of literature which raised Faust to the status of an enduring archetype of the human condition.

The Faust legend had spread across Europe in the late sixteenth century, and an English-language version was produced in 1592. This was almost certainly the source for Christopher Marlowe's *Dr Faustus*. In this play, unquestionably Marlowe's greatest (and an intimation of what might have been if he had not been killed at the age of 29 in a Deptford pub brawl), he lifts the Faust legend out of primitive Lutheranism into the Renaissance.

Marlowe's Faust is a restless creature who knows that know-ledge is power and wealth. His boundless thirst for experience and domination leads him on. In Marlowe's hands, Faust becomes a titanic figure, determined to bestride the world at any cost. Even Mephistopheles, the servant of Lucifer, the Devil, tries to talk him out of his ambition at first, to no avail: he burns his bridges and signs the contract which gives him twenty-four years of earthly fulfilment, in return for his soul:

> Had I as many souls as there are stars,
> I'd give them all for Mephistopheles.
> By him I'll be great emperor of the world.

A rumbustuous cavalcade follows. Yet all is not well. An old man appeals to Faust to recognize what course he is on. He almost listens. But the addiction gets the better of him again, and as the drama moves to its climax he demands to 'glut the longing of my heart's desire' in an encounter with the ideal of perfect feminine beauty – Helen of Troy. This encounter is his mountain top, his moment of fulfilment, the moment when the Devil delivers fully on his part in the contract:

> Was this the face that launch'd a thousand ships?
> And burnt the topless towers of Ilium?
> Sweet Helen, make me immortal with a kiss.
> Her lips suck forth my soul: see, where it flies! –
> Come, Helen, come, give me my soul again.
> Here will I dwell, for heaven is in these lips,
> And all is dross that is not Helena.

From this there is no return. Faust is possessed – not so much by something that is trivial and worthless as by something that is not real. The play ends with a powerfully dramatized, but conventional, finale in which the clock strikes midnight and an agonized Faust is taken away to hell.

What is already, in the hands of Marlowe, a parable of the new human inquisitive/acquisitive drive becomes even richer, subtler and much more ambiguous in Goethe's extraordinary masterpiece.

Goethe spent much of a lifetime on his *Faust*. When he began work on the concept, in the early 1770s, he was in his twenties. He completed the whole work in 1832, only months before the end of

a long life. He was unaware of Marlowe's play until he was well
advanced on the project. Over half a century, the drama evolved
into a two-part magnum opus, over 12,000 lines long (eight times
the length of Marlowe's play). If Marlowe's *Faust* is a Renaissance
titan, Goethe's *Faust* is a giant driven by the Enlightenment. It is
rarely performed in full, because of its sheer scale and complexity.
I saw Peter Stein's production in Berlin in 2004: the performance was
spread over a weekend and the impact was unforgettable. In its
grandeur it is reminiscent of Wagner; in its richly varied content and
style it has the genius of Shakespeare; and in its post-Enlightenment
open-endedness it resonates with a twenty-first-century human spirit
that knows what heights it can scale and what depths it can plumb.

Goethe's Faust focuses crucially not on a contract but on a wager.
Weary of bookish study, like Marlowe's Faust, he yearns for action
and experience. But in his negotiations with Mephistopheles he
insists on a crucial condition:

> If ever I say to the moment:
> But stay awhile – O, how beautiful you are!
> Then you may clap me in irons,
> Then I will happily be brought down,
> Then may the death knell sound,
> Then you are free from your service.

Far more sophisticated than a simple contract, this is a challenge to
Mephistopheles to provide even just one moment of pure fulfilment.
It is the basis for an extraordinary journey in search of experience.
Will it ever include a moment which meets this test?

The journey he embarks on has its share of buffoonery, as in
Marlowe. But it is far more embracing in its scope. It includes
the tragedy of Gretchen: Faust's seduction of an innocent young
woman, their love-making, then his abrupt abandonment of her
when she becomes pregnant. As the story unfolds in painful intensity
and she goes to her death for the murder of her baby, she grows in
stature while he is diminished.

But he continues his journey, and as he does so he becomes less a
specific flesh-and-blood human, and more a symbolic figure. Not

Everyman, but a figure representing the aspirations of the great man of action, who is not content with philosophizing or with time-serving, but whose urge is to experience and have an effect on the world, using Mephistopheles's services as he goes. Goethe's Faust has Napoleonic characteristics, as well as echoes in Marx (in his famous critique of uninvolved learning: 'Philosophers seek to understand the world: the point, however, is to change it'). He becomes almost the spirit of the age which had already dawned by the eighteenth century and which reached its high noon in the twentieth: restless, this-worldly, enquiring, domineering, acquisitive, action-oriented.

Goethe's *Faust* is almost unbelievably full of allusion and allegory. After the tragedy of Gretchen, in the lengthy second part of the drama Faust continues his journey through scenes which are an allegory of the corrupt and decadent world of *ancien régime* Europe in the seventeenth and eighteenth centuries (including a fascinatingly prescient scene in which Mephistopheles enables a feckless ruler to deal with his financial straits by printing money and precipitating inflation); through a voyage of discovery around a representation of classical Greece (but can humanity ever achieve satisfaction by looking backwards to an alleged golden age?); through his central encounter with Helen of Troy (in whom he discovers a bliss which, in contrast to Marlowe's Faust, he seems to know cannot endure, because it is ideal and unreal, not part of tempestuous reality); through a return to the real world which plunges into what is in effect an allegory of the upheavals of a nineteenth-century Europe convulsed by the after-effects of the French Revolution; and then to the final denouement and Faust's extraordinary apotheosis (quite the opposite of Marlowe's climactic moment of damnation).

The last act of this huge tableau of the modern human spirit has Faust undertaking a project which at one level seems banal after the superhuman struggles of earlier scenes, and at another level is an emblem of the human desire to engineer the world, to reshape it for its own purposes. Faust's project to drain marshland and make it fit for human prosperity gives him finally a satisfaction at the end of a long life of searching (he is symbolically a hundred years old), such that he cries out to Mephistopheles, even as death is about to catch up with him:

> To stand on free ground with people who are free!
> In that moment I could say
> 'But stay awhile – O, how beautiful you are!
> The trace of my earthly days
> Will never be lost through eons of time' –
> This foretaste of great happiness
> Is now my greatest moment.

Mephistopheles has in effect lost his wager. Faust's admission is not only conditional, but is triggered by the prospect of something which will create human well-being, not by a moment of self-gratification.

There follows a strange, ambiguous apotheosis. Mephistopheles is rebuffed, and the soul of Faust is taken up into a heaven where the figure of God seems absent, but where the Mater Gloriosa, the Queen of Heaven of Catholic piety, receives him and he is transformed and redeemed (as Gretchen has been). Goethe was in no sense a conventional Christian. But this vivid, mysterious ending is certainly not pure irony. His (unorthodox) use of the iconography of grace and redemption is ambivalent and open-ended, as is the very final 'mystical chorus':

> Everything transient
> Is only an image;
> The unattainable
> Is happening;
> What cannot be described
> Is now done;
> The eternal feminine
> Draws us on.

Faust is a figure for the modern age. Goethe was profoundly ambivalent about what was unfolding in his day (and would have been appalled by where it led to in the twentieth century). His 'hero' reflects that ambivalence. As an eminent British scholar of his work, John R. Williams, put it: '[Faust's] idealism is qualified by his daemonic ruthlessness, his satisfaction in achievement is limited by his obsessive covetousness, his altruism is vitiated by his impatience, his prosperity by his crimes, and even his final utopian vision is subverted by a profound irony.' In the end, Mephistopheles loses his hold on Faust. Yet the final transformation offers a hope which is not a simple overlooking of all that has happened, and whose basis and implications are left beguilingly unclear.

Goethe's *Faust* seems almost uncontrolled in its luxuriance. Goethe himself more or less explicitly recognized its centrifugal tendencies and open-endedness. The work's rich allusiveness and allegorical power have spawned a whole industry of literary criticism. Goethe himself time and again refused to be pinned down about its specific meanings. Perhaps, as with all the greatest works of art, its openness to interpretation is a mark of its genius.

Its enduring relevance in the globalized world of the twenty-first century lies surely in the ambiguity of Faust's experience, in the ambiguity of his flawed final triumph, and in the strange ambiguity of his apotheosis. In the Gretchen story, we see the tragedy of the abuse of the vulnerable. But whose tragedy is it? Just Gretchen's? Or also Faust's? In Helen of Troy we see the temptation (and the impossibility) of escape from reality into the realm of ideals and the idyllic. For you can't live in pleasure groves and be fulfilled; you have to deal in inconvenient realities. And, in the end, satisfaction seems to come – even for the unscrupulous bully – in getting something prosaically material done. What an irony for the man who sets out with limitless ambition to be the colossus of history. (Is this the fate that inevitably befalls politicians in our times?)

And, all the while, Mephistopheles is there: that sense of the presence of evil which at least reminds us of the seriousness of what is at stake. Even in a world which has lost the fear that demons are lurking round every corner, even in a world which finds it hard to hold on to moral absolutes, we retain a sense of the presence of evil. It remains an important source of our discomfort with ourselves.

And then there is that final apotheosis. What is the basis for the redemption that Faust is offered? Where is God anyway? Whatever this all means, it is plainly *not* simply validation of Faust's human striving to assert himself. And what exactly does that final mystical chorus tell us? What is the 'eternal feminine' that 'draws us on'? (But that is a question for the final chapter.)

It is clear that, in the hands of Goethe, Faust has travelled a long way from the simple morality play of the sixteenth century. At the core of Goethe's drama is the archetype of the individual who asserts self by doing and having. To be more is the alternative to being nothing: and to be more is to do more and have more. There is a price to pay, but it is a price the individual pays knowingly – at least in part. So it is an archetype which has more and more resonance as the human consciousness becomes more and more individualized, under the impact of globalization.

It should be no surprise that the Faustian bargain recurs again and again in literature through the centuries. The individual – either larger than life or would-be larger than life – who pays the price is an enduring motif. Shakespeare (in whose plays it is said that you can find every human instinct, thought or feeling) offers us one perfect example: Macbeth. In a moving soliloquy of doubt and hesitation before Duncan's murder, he muses:

> If it were done when 'tis done, then 'twere well
> It were done quickly. If the assassination
> Could trammel up the consequence, and catch
> With his surcease success; that but this blow
> Might be the be-all and the end-all here –
> But here upon this bank and shoal of time –
> We'd jump the life to come . . .

This is the Faustian bargain. Urged on by his wife, Macbeth takes it on: the bargain in which he sells his soul to take power, to 'make history'. Not many people do this in the grand manner. But far too many people sacrifice too much to ambition and power. And – perhaps – the more mundane the objective, the easier it is to deceive ourselves about what we are doing.

There are other ways too of settling for a bargain with what always turns out to be a lesser god. Worship of the pleasure principle is another, of which Don Giovanni is the classic example. This most powerful of Mozart's heroes blazes a trail of female 'conquests' – to use the eighteenth-century euphemism – that takes him, via the murder of the Commendatore, to the confrontation with his victim's statue in the graveyard, to his refusal to repent or mend his ways, to damnation. To some, his very defiance is cause for sneaking admiration – as if he were some kind of Promethean hero thumbing his nose at the gods (or an existentialist hero who accepts his end as inevitable but not as punishment). But he is in truth the epitome of the utterly selfish pleasure-seeker, and has implicitly made the Faustian bargain. And how many people do that? Again, the more mundane the prize, the less obvious, perhaps, is the price.

Then there is the temptation to seek creative fame (and/or wealth) at the expense of real creativity. One of the short stories of Nikolai Gogol, published in his collection *Arabesques* in 1835 and called 'The Portrait', tells the story of a young, classically poor artist in St Petersburg. He is fascinated by a strange, apparently unfinished, portrait of an unknown man in an Asiatic robe, which he finds in an art dealer's shop. The eyes of the man seem to fix themselves on him. He buys the picture with his last twenty copecks, and then cannot pay the rent on his garret. In nightmarish slumber, he seems to see the man step from the frame and drop rolls of money on the ground, one of which he sneaks away. He awakes to find real money rolled up and hidden in the frame. He resolves to use the new freedom from care and want this gives him to develop his creative talent; but instead he develops a taste for the comfortable life, and a career making more money by doing fashionable society portraits of no artistic merit. But he goes insane with jealousy when a poor pupil produces work which wins real acclaim from the art critics.

The second part of this eerie story focuses on the origins of the portrait in a strange commission to a local artist by a moneylender in a far-off village who was thought to have trafficked with the Devil. Despite the artist's unease, the moneylender begs him to complete the picture: he seems to sense that he will be doomed if he dies before it is finished. Yet he does die, and the unfinished portrait unsettles the minds of all who own it.

Gogol's story resonates with a growing nineteenth-century super-naturalism of a kind that would have felt out of place in the eighteenth-century mindset of Goethe and even of Mozart. But, though the guise is different, the Faustian theme is clearly detectible. Chartkov, the artist, sells out his creative urge for money, respectability and comfort. How many of us, one way or another, do the same?

Yet another guise of the Faustian bargain is displayed in another story of a portrait – this one much better known to the English-speaking world: Oscar Wilde's *The Picture of Dorian Gray*, published in 1891. The young Dorian's wish for his portrait to age in his stead is the sinister basis for a life of eternal youth, lived in the selfish pursuit of beauty. The echoes of Faust are striking: Dorian's rejection destroys a young actress in an obvious parallel to the Gretchen tragedy; he embarks on a serious of vices, becoming inter alia a frequent visitor to an opium den; there is even a point of remorse – or rather taking stock – as in Marlowe's *Faust*, but not real guilt. And all the while he preserves his extraordinary youth and beauty, while the portrait ages. The denouement as he slashes the portrait – only to fall dead, aged and withered – is Wilde's *fin de siècle* alternative to Marlowe's damnation scene.

Wilde's story is partly about the pursuit of the pleasure principle (à la *Don Giovanni*); but it is also, classically, about the refusal to age, the denial of mortality. And what is more characteristic of today's spirit than that? In ways ranging from the trivial and obvious to the subtle and indirect, so many succumb to this urge. It is of course the psychological basis of the cosmetic-surgery industry; it manifests itself too in the often obsessive pursuit of fitness and dietary health. More significantly, it lies behind the determination of many a political or business leader to hang on for too long, wallowing in the conviction that no successor is yet ready. And, more generally, we feed this obsession in society at large by treating long life as a virtue (or even a reward) rather than as a gift.

Faust and the ambition for power; Faust and the pursuit of pleasure; Faust and the monetization of creative genius; Faust and the quest for eternal youth. He has many variants – as many as the ways in which human beings struggle to assert themselves.

And what of the figure of Mephistopheles, the servant of his ambitions? In the world of the urbanized global market, in which we are all increasingly both connected and individualized, it is surely money which becomes the modern Mephistopheles. As economics teaches us, money is both a means of exchange and a store of value. As philosophers have noted, its role as store of value elides into an embodiment of value itself. The means become an end. The lubricating mechanism of investment, production and commerce becomes its own goal. The servant risks becoming the master.

We can see this happening at the level of nation states down the centuries since the Spanish began importing gold into Europe. The mercantilist urge to accumulate gold (and, later, currency reserves) continues to distort international economic relationships into the twenty-first century. Economists and politicians debate the policy issues posed by the global financial imbalances which are the result. We should not forget that these imbalances reflect a deeply rooted human tendency as well.

It is a tendency which operates pervasively in the individual psyche. Money is potentially liberating: it breaks down social barriers, and enables conventions to be flouted for good and for ill. It is the servant which enables us to pursue our dreams. What in the world of Macbeth or Don Giovanni was limited to the aristocracy, and in the world of Goethe's Faust or Gogol or Wilde to the world of art and the literati, is now increasingly democratized. More and more of us can make the Faustian bargain, and put ourselves in the hands of the modern Mephistopheles. You no longer have to be a titan to do it.

Which brings us to the story of the rich young man. In his time he is an establishment figure. Now his equivalents generally see themselves as middle class. Nameless, but successful and well-heeled, he seems nevertheless to be conscious that all is not well. He is not a man who is ready to say to the passing moment, 'But stay awhile ...' He encounters a teacher who is becoming known for being provocative – even disturbing, to say the least – and asks what he should do to inherit eternal life (and – though unstated – find his peace). The teacher's answer is conventional for the times: keep the moral law, as embodied in the Ten Commandments. The rich young man responds that he has done this from his youth onward (and perhaps he believes he has). At which point the teacher turns to him and to his real need. This story is told more or less identically in the gospel narratives of Matthew, Mark and Luke. But Mark's version has a telling gloss (unusually since Mark, almost universally regarded as the earliest of the evangelists, is generally sparing of detail, reflection or interpretation). The teacher 'looked at him, *loved him*, and said: "One thing you lack; take your treasure, sell it and give the proceeds to the poor, and come follow me. And you will have treasure in heaven."'

This is *ad personam*, addressed to a particular man who has a particular need. This is a man addicted to his money as an alcoholic is to drink. And the remedy proposed by the teacher is essentially the same as for any addict: begin by acknowledging what you are; then you can escape into a new life which will be richer than you were able to imagine.

One way of describing the young man's problem is that he has in fact broken one of those commandments he claims to have kept – one that no self-respecting establishment figure of his time would have considered breaking, and which he would certainly not have accepted that he had broken. The second commandment is a ban on the worship of lesser gods, of idols. But he is possessed by his money, which he thought he himself possessed. He has come to worship his money; his money has become his god.

Another way of putting the point is that he has made the Faustian bargain, and the servant has become the master. Whatever way we look at it, the story has a poignant ending. The man ducks the challenge and turns away – and leaves no further trace. He is in thrall to his servant.

All this is not just a voyage of literary exploration. Faust and the rich young man speak to the real condition of large numbers of people –

at all times and in all places, and certainly in the early twenty-first century when so many are so busy in the global bazaar. We live in a world where increasingly everything is for sale – including ourselves.

So how do we avoid the trap? Opt out to avoid the risk of contamination? But if opting out means living a comfortable existence away from the madding crowd on unearned income, then it's romantic nonsense to imagine that this could ever be an option for more than a pampered few. And in any case, such self-indulgence carries within it the seeds of boredom, dissatisfaction and vacuousness. There are, of course, other paths to choose which may appear to be opting out but which are in reality the reverse. I have stayed on Mount Athos with monks who have chosen to spend the rest of their lives there. For retreat and spiritual refreshment amid natural beauty and a profusion of icons and frescoes which have seen centuries go by, Mount Athos is unsurpassed. But no one would regard the desire to escape the world of money and commerce as remotely sufficient a motive for a lifetime there. Retreat to the mountain top is one thing: life on the mountain is an intensely different matter.

What, then, about the path taken by my ex-banker friend in Kolkata? Isn't that the route that the rich young man is being challenged to follow?

Well, it may be. But the challenge to the rich young man is *ad personam*. His experience does not mean that money can *never* be a true servant – only that we need to be aware of the responsibilities and the risks that it carries. Whether we should follow a path out of the world of money as he is called on to do must be a question for the individual. And it is certainly clear that such a path – with all its discomforts and potential risks – can never be just an opt-out. Those who take it feel drawn to it, not simply repelled by the road more travelled. Those I know who have taken this path and kept going on it are transparently in their element and as engaged in the world as any aggressive trader.

In any case, it is a path which can be taken only by a minority. The fact is that human welfare and development depend on most of us being involved in one way or another in productive exchange.

This is what creates the surplus which supports Mount Athos, or Future Hope, or the Familia Moja Children's Centre (not to mention pensions, educational services, medical care and social services on our doorsteps).

And, as previous chapters have argued, that productive exchange takes place in a global marketplace to which, for all its imperfections, there is no realistic alternative. Many of us have no alternative but to make our way there, living and working in all the ambiguity and imperfection (including our own).

Recognizing and accepting this pervasive moral ambiguity is crucial: otherwise we never get engaged, or we break, or we make a sinister bargain. This acceptance helps us do more than survive. If we want to see life as more than just 'one damn thing after another', we have to begin by seeing we are part of what makes it what it is. We ourselves are both source and victim of these imperfections. We can see that we are caught in the spider's web, and we have to start from there.

One of the great dangers of having no tolerance for the ambiguity of imperfection is the temptation to go for the Faustian option. The Faustian option is the bargain that grants immediate and undiluted pleasure/power/sex/money in exchange for acceptance of the consequences, whatever they are. We take this option in many small ways all the time, and sometimes we justify it because we can't bear the ambiguity of imperfection. Why struggle with a difficult and obdurate challenge that is never really going to be solved, when we could forget all about it and go shopping instead? Yet the bargain is illusory. It turns out that we don't get satisfaction that way either. The pleasure of it just melts in our hands. Hence the pervasive fact of imperfection that seems to bedevil our spirits one way or another – whether we are trying to leave a monument behind us or whether we just want speedboats.

So we need to commit to the challenge, for all the ambiguity it involves. And, as we do so, we will learn that we can avoid the Faustian risk and keep to a path of fulfilment if and only if we are prepared to follow certain guiding principles. These principles are not new – any more than the clichés about money or the legend of

Faust are new. In one sense, there is nothing new under the sun; in another sense, the era of globalization has given these principles a greater relevance for more people, and a greater urgency, than at any previous stage in human history.

The first of these principles is simply that of integrity. As argued in Chapters 5 and 6 in respect of businesses, values matter to (long-term) value. For the individual, the parallel principle is that values matter to real satisfaction in working life. This raises the question, What values? Are they different from one culture to another? If so, who is to determine which are the right ones? Can we really say that there is a universal standard of integrity for the world of commerce, when it is precisely the meeting point of every creed, culture and community under the sun?

But this line of questioning has more of the debating tactic about it than any practical significance. For what is striking about life in the global bazaar is just how widespread the consensus is about what it takes to do ethical business. Individuals, as well as whole cultures, can and do disagree on profoundly important moral questions: on abortion, on voluntary euthanasia, on the possibilities inherent in stem-cell research, on habeas corpus as applied to terror suspects – and so on. At a different level, philosophers may choose to debate whether there are any moral absolutes or universals at all – and, if so, what makes them so and how we recognize them. But as a matter of fact the ethics of the marketplace are almost by definition universal, not so much because of some agreed metaphysical truth, but because of the practicalities of doing business on a sustainable basis – and because of the realities of human psychology. Everyone knows about the importance of trust and honesty for sustainable business. Everyone knows that, though you can fool some people all of the time and most people some of the time, you can't fool most people most of the time. Human psychology tells us of course that many will try. But human psychology also tells us – virtually all of us – that this is no way to the enduring success or recognition or fulfilment which most people at some level or other yearn for, for that comes only with an integrity based on honesty, trust and a real desire to exchange value for value.

Other guiding principles could be said to follow from this one. And they are worth spelling out, because they cumulatively enlarge the implications of this first principle of integrity to the point where it embraces the whole person. We learn as we go that integrity in the global bazaar is about something much more than *just* the global bazaar.

Thus, secondly, the way of fulfilment is clearly one which treats others (colleagues or customers) as ends, not just as means. Both as ends and as means, the human relationships of the workplace are of course important, and in a world of uncertainty and market competition it is naive to imagine that responsibility for them will not sometimes pose painful dilemmas. But we all know also that the history of organizational life is littered with examples of those who manipulate, who pick up and discard, who flatter to deceive, and who run organizations purely by numbers (when they are in fact organisms, not just organizations). And we know too that this is the way to a feared, or despised, and lonely end.

Ambition, thirdly, is entirely consistent with fulfilment – real fulfilment – if it is ambition to contribute the most, not to get the most. Nor is ambition necessarily vitiated by being competitive (which is made highly likely given the inevitably pyramidal nature of leadership in so much of organized human endeavour). Competitive ambition becomes destructive only to the extent that it jettisons the above principle that colleagues are ends not just means; and all ambition becomes destructive when the goal becomes the be-all and end-all of life (and that phrase, with its origins in Macbeth, should alert us to the Faustian threat).

Which leads directly to a fourth principle: human beings have a need, and a responsibility, to balance their commitments to different realms of living. These different realms normally overlap: their borders are blurred. These are the realms of family, of work, of friendships and of wider social groupings – and of the inner self. The interrelationship between these realms takes as many forms as there are human beings – the more so in a globalized world of inter-connection and individualization. Whole books can be – have been – written on what makes for a healthy balance among them. What matters for the present purpose, however, is not so much the pre-scription for health – which we should expect to be as varied as people are – but simply the recognition of this balance as crucial to fulfilment and the avoidance of the Faustian trap.

Then, fifthly, there is a vital principle of leadership. It is for business or organizational psychologists to analyse what personal profiles make for successful leadership. But recent years have seen growing recognition of the value of what is sometimes called 'servant leadership' – leadership whose essence is not psychological domin-ation, but which seeks to share itself, to set an example, to instil the instinct of leadership in others, and thus to serve the common endeavour. At its best, such leadership knows full well that it cannot shirk the responsibilities of decision-making and must often take risks in this (including risks to its own popularity). But it also recognizes the leadership – the contribution – of others. It sees every person as having leadership responsibilities and potential, whatever their position in an organization chart and whether or not they have anyone reporting to them, for everyone is in a position to influence others, for good or for ill. Seen as domination, leadership im-poverishes both the leader and the led; seen as service in this way, it enriches both, and is more enduringly effective.

Finally, there is a crucial principle which underpins all the above, and which is too often ignored in all the books on how to get on in life. We need to be able to look ourselves in the mirror and ask two questions about our role in the global bazaar: How is what I am doing contributing to human welfare? And why specifically am I doing it? These questions matter because of the demands made on us by our work. It may not be – should not be – the be-all or end-all of our life; but it is not just a hobby either. For the majority of us, work consumes much or even most of our creative energy and potential. This is too high a price for us to tell ourselves we are just doing it for the money. Nor is it enough to tell ourselves we do it because we can excel in it, or because we have drifted into it, or because we are trapped in it and are serving time. Any of these answers may be true for our particular circumstances; none of them satisfies. Neither money nor ambition nor serendipity is good enough as a work/life principle. We have to find a better answer to the question: Why do I do what I do? – which is really this two-part question: What value is it, and why am I doing it (as opposed to somebody else)?

The answer matters. We have only one life. And at any given point we have only three options for our way forward, for our involvement in the bazaar: the Faustian bargain which puts self at the centre; drift; and the search for contribution. And drift is no answer, any more than is the Faustian bargain. Drift is the opposite of the Faustian risk. Since drifters do not try to reach to the stars, they do not crash to earth. There is no danger of their being able to say, 'But stay awhile . . .' They may perhaps find fulfilment in other realms of life, but not in the work that takes up so much of their time. Drift is a way to desiccation of the spirit, and often to low-level depression. No help from Mephistopheles is needed on such a course.

The crucial truth is that only one of the three options offers a way to fulfilment. So we have to be able to answer these questions: What is the value of what I do? And does it use my gifts and my interests? Does it stimulate me, stretch me, challenge me, teach me? Because if not, why exactly am I doing it?

To be clear, the contribution we make will never be unambiguous. It will often be indirect, and always be flawed. But the questions are there, as generic and specific ones, for each individual. Can the engineer see why her bridge designs contribute to human welfare? Can the banker see why his trade finance business does the same? Or the retailer? Or the corporate lawyer? Or the treasury civil servant? Or the hip specialist? And so on. Where are the invisible boundaries between different shades of grey, between that which contributes and that which is destructive? Much of the time, just asking the question is salutary. Being able to say to the face in the mirror that, taken in the large, the area of activity and the role I play in it contributes – albeit imperfectly – to the development of human welfare; this is a necessary condition for fulfilment. (Necessary, of course, but not sufficient: motives and behaviour count too.) The alternative – not being able to say at least this much – is a warning signal we ignore at the peril of the wholeness of our being.

There is of course far more to be said *ad personam* to ourselves and to others as individuals. There are crucial points in life when the questions become acute: for young people as they emerge at the threshold of working life; for those in mid-career who are faced with a crossroads for whatever reason – whether the break-through job offer or, alternatively, redundancy (which used to be as rare as divorce once was, and is now as common as divorce has become). And, in these days of longer life expectancy and healthier older years, maybe the questions even present themselves on the threshold of so-called retirement. Are we really going to find fulfilment in a twenty-year period of golf and tourism? Are there not contributions we can still make? Are there not in fact new options to do so directly, rather than in the indirect way that an earlier stage of life in the workplace may have demanded?

The questions are there too at points of spectacular failure. What happens when the young CEO of a public company, who has been used to nothing but success in everything he does, is forced out because an acquisition goes wrong and drags down the share price? What happens when a young trader in a bank dealing room covers up his losses with fictitious transactions until they spiral out of control and into the limelight? What happens to the up-and-coming politician brought down by a financial impropriety or a sexual misdemeanour? Or to the social worker who misses the evidence of child abuse that leads to a death? And so on. The rest of us may often have cause to say, 'There but the grace of God ...'. But the individual – what does he or she do? There is a whole variety of responses, of course: total or partial denial (it was not my fault; others were to blame too); or depression and loss of self-esteem; even suicide. Some go hard; others flee (others avoid themselves); yet others implode.

But there's always another way: there is always the possibility of redemption. John Profumo, a British politician of the early 1960s, famously found his career at an abrupt end after a colourful sex scandal; his redemption came as he quietly went to work for a community-work charity in east London. He ended up running it, and then retiring with honours and respect. What does it take to follow such a path? Coming to terms with yourself and what you have done, for a start; then sensing that you owe something. And then learning through experience that in paying this debt you receive far more than you ever imagined possible in your former life.

And so on. The (rewarding) irony is, furthermore, that as we ask these questions of ourselves and strive to face up to the answers, we enrich our experience of life (which is precisely what Faust sought to do). We continue to learn and grow. We can – need to – learn from what we do wrong, from the mistakes we make, from the failures we suffer. We learn from these experiences to the extent that we are able to offer and accept forgiveness and self-forgiveness. And in the search we may glimpse what Faust is seeking and is doomed never to find – what T. S. Eliot calls 'a lifetime burning in every moment'.

One way of describing the prize is completeness – the opposite of that dangerous compartmentalization which divides life into different realms with different rules, and which is the besetting sin of the global bazaar.

And yet to describe the prize in that way is to risk the suggestion that it is perfectly achievable. Which is wrong. Completeness is the unachievable goal. All the above is easier said than done – or rather lived. And we know we will often stumble. We can hope to converge to the goal; we know we will often diverge from it. But it is no accident that the Faust legend includes moments when he could have broken free. In truth, there are always such moments. So we can indeed hope to converge, though not to arrive. But we *can* always hope.

8

In My End is My Beginning

Not, I'll not, carrion comfort, Despair, not feast on thee;
Not untwist – slack they may be – these last strands of man
In me or, most weary, cry I can no more. I can;
Can something, hope, wish day come, not choose not to be.
Gerard Manley Hopkins, 'Carrion Comfort' (1885)

In my beginning is my end.
In my end is my beginning.
T. S. Eliot 'East Coker' (1941),
first and last words

The goal is a completeness we will never fully achieve; but the journey is all-important. The end is clear, and it defines how we must begin. Completeness in our lives – the avoidance of that compartmentalization which is spiritually and morally so dangerous – involves starting with the acceptance of the ambiguities of life: the ambiguity which arises from the fact that all our experience is shot through with a striking and seemingly unavoidable degree of imperfection; the ambiguity about the nature of the end of human development; and that strange principle of hope which seems irrational and yet is capable of giving light in all manner of circumstances.

We need to recognize these ambiguities as we seek to interpret our history, evaluate our experience, and weigh the life choices we and others make. And if we are to do so honestly, with integrity, and in search of healing and learning, then we have to become aware of the biases which distort our insight. This is true at two levels: first, in our perspective on history and society, on 'the world out there'; and, second, in our own self-understanding. We all of us have biases on both levels; we may or may not be able to remove them entirely, but we should at least aim to be aware of them.

So far as 'the world out there' is concerned, for instance, Europeans far too readily see human history through a Eurocentric lens. Why is it, for example, that they will typically know at least something about Alexander the Great – arguably the first powerful leader of European history – but almost nothing about the first emperor of China, even though his importance in global history was by any objective measure as great? Conversely, the Chinese world view is revealed in the very name by which the country is known – the Middle Kingdom. Meanwhile, the idea of Manifest Destiny still to this day underlies America's view of itself and feeds what strikes Europeans as a remarkable and quasi-religious patriotism. We may or may not want to shed these perspectives, but we will certainly gain in understanding by becoming aware of alternatives. And as we do so, we will begin to recognize those ambiguities about human development the more clearly.

Then there is our own self-understanding, with its inevitable distortions. 'Now I see through a glass darkly . . . now I know in part . . .' Much of the distortion comes from childhood, of course. 'The child is father of the man.' That is why the toboggan named 'Rosebud' is such a powerful icon. It is given to very few of us to be free of baggage from the years before we could reflect and form our own perspective – from our beginnings. Some of us are obviously fighting demons from childhood for the rest of our days. 'In a clearing stands a boxer/ And a fighter by his trade . . .' – yet fighting not 'by his trade', but rather with his past. Some are aware of it, yet cannot help themselves; others are not even aware of what they are wrestling with.

Again, there are those whose childhood has knocked the stuffing out of them. There are so many ways for this to happen – as many as there are children who are abused, who learn that they are disappointments to their parents, or who are discouraged rather than encouraged in a thousand ways. One way or another, self-esteem fails to blossom, and the ambiguities and reversals of life become a reinforcing chain of unfulfilled discontent and even despair.

Even the happiest families – where there are many memories of colour and life and love, such that recollections are tinged with melancholy for the lost past rather than anger at it – leave distortions. In fact it can come as something of a surprise to the adult to realize that the father or mother you miss had feet of clay for one reason or another, and that this has left its imprint – however light – on your own psychology. In a happy family, that discovery may be one made in love and understanding (for the baggage they in turn carried, that gave them feet of clay); but it is not less a self-discovery for that. (As an aside, there is no famous opening of a great novel less true than the first sentence of Tolstoy's *Anna Karenina* – 'All happy families are happy in the same way; each unhappy family is unhappy in its own special way'.)

One way or another, the more we recognize our own biases and distortions – about the world and in ourselves – the more clearly we come to recognize the ambiguities of life: the imperfection, the uncertainty, and yet the potential of hope. And the better our chances on the journey.

But however fully we own up to – and perhaps even set aside – our cultural biases and psychological distortions, and so deepen our insight, we nevertheless interpret and judge our experience though a prism. We cannot avoid this. Pure 'objectivity', meaning uninterpreted, unevaluated description of the flow of human affairs of which we are a part, is effectively impossible. For we see inevitably through the prism of a metaphysical and moral framework. Our prism is a metaphysical one in that it reflects our understanding of the origin, nature and value of being (and beings). And it is a moral framework in that we cannot avoid judgement – not just valuation, but evaluation.

This prism of ours may be a specific set of religious beliefs entailing an explicit and elaborate moral code. It may be a set of religious beliefs implying some broader moral principles – rather than a detailed code – which we strive to make applicable to specific situations of life. It may alternatively be a set of moral principles devised from our own judgement and reflections, without any religious basis – because we are either agnostic or atheist (with implications accordingly for our metaphysical framework). And these moral principles may be based on a detailed ideology about the way societies should be, or they may be minimalist and laissez-faire. Alternatively of course, our moral prism may be one of pure self-interest – the amoral principle (allied either to an atheistic metaphysics or, Faust-like, to a metaphysical reality we seek to control).

Some people can articulate their metaphysics: some religious people do, atheists do, humanists often do. Many don't or can't. Some people think out their moral principles consciously and rationally. Many others live with moral frameworks that are inherited from previous generations and are often only partly recognized for what they are and where they come from. Usually our moral framework is related, at least partly, to our metaphysical framework. But not necessarily. There is plenty of scope for compartmentalization here: too often there is an obvious disconnection between what is said in worship (of whatever) and what is done in life. And conversely, as plenty of agnostics and atheists will claim, the metaphysical assumption that all is mere chance in the universe need be no logical barrier to setting a demanding moral groundwork for life.

Whatever is the case, at root we are all bound to believe in the universal validity of our metaphysical framework, and in the universal applicability of our moral groundwork. We may well recognize that we cannot prove this definitively and to the satisfaction of everyone else. We may well recognize the deep conviction of others' metaphysics or moral groundwork. We will surely assert their right to hold their views in the realm of metaphysics, and on moral issues too – so long as they do not impinge on ourselves or on society at large. But we cannot with integrity think and act as if our own metaphysical framework were not of profound relevance, or as if our moral groundwork were purely relative.

This is true virtually by definition. Our metaphysical framework is a prism through which we interpret all history and experience (both human history as a whole and our own history in particular). It is our metaphysical framework which tells us whether that history has any more value than the history of colonies of ants, or even of the tide coming in and out. It provides our answer to the question as to why, and how far, that history is significant. And on the basis of some answer to that question, we interpret – make judgements about – success or failure, potential and purpose, progress or decay. There is effectively no such thing as objectively describable human history and experience, i.e. without such interpretation and judgement in terms of our chosen metaphysical framework. So to see ourselves and our history is to see through a prism: to see is to interpret, and to interpret is to see from the perspective of a metaphysical framework.

And just as we are bound to see the world through such a metaphysical prism, so we cannot with integrity treat our moral groundwork as purely relative – as applying only to ourselves, or to our culture, or to our age. To do so is effectively a contradiction in terms. We hold, for example, that slavery is evil, even though almost every major culture in history has allowed it and justified it. This is an absolute judgement. We hold that infanticide is wrong, even though numerous societies throughout history down to the present day have practised it (or even required it in the context of ritual sacrifice); we cannot accept that this judgement is socially or culturally relative. We take the same view about serfdom, about suttee, about foot-binding – or, to take an apparently more mundane example from the world of commerce, about contracts: a contract is a contract even if oral. Such truths we hold to be universal.

Of course, we are not sure how far we can take this. We know that society's view of what is right has evolved over time on so many topics. We also know that such views can vary – at least somewhat – from one culture to another. We know that on some topics – on abortion, for example – there is passionate disagreement. We will often have cause to acknowledge our own inconsistency and/or that our own views tend to evolve in the light of experience. So our moral judgements often need to be flavoured with a large dose of humility and doubt.

But none of this alters the basic point that the sense of universal validity is intrinsic to the very meaning of a moral groundwork – just as universal relevance is of the very essence of our metaphysical framework. And this has consequences for us. Because, for the sake of our integrity and our spiritual well-being, we need to avoid compartmentalization. We need to connect our metaphysical and moral framework – what we worship, what we admire, what we hold dear, what we hold to be right – with what we think about the world and what we do and should do. None of the realms we move in – our family life, our social life, our work life – is neutral ground.

In this sense, my interpretive prism is Christian. This is not the place for a full explanation of what that means to me. If I tried to write a full credo, I would fail: I am not a theologian, and in any case, I do not know what a full credo could be. I was once asked by a business friend to summarize what I believe in ten bullet points. I tried, but didn't like the result. Ten bullet points, ten assertions: they were at once too many and too few – too many cut-and-dried statements; too few for the varied learnings from and about life. Bullet points discourage questions, moreover. And questions (meaning questions without an answer, questions that have no answer, questions that are the pathways of mystery) are the antithesis of the decisive business life that summarizes issues in bullet points. A fortiori, bullet points discourage doubts. But, though doubts are the apparent antithesis of the religious life, how many people could honestly say that they have none?

What I believe, though, is part of me. But I have too much uncertainty to be a fundamentalist. And I could no more be an atheist than a fundamentalist, for amid the cloud of unknowing I also get glimpses of certainty – unpredictable, transient, and hard to articulate. Showing my frail mother a photograph of my long-dead grandmother in her youth alongside one of my daughters, and seeing the indefinable similarity of expression bring tears to her eyes. Drinking a glass of wine on a Friday evening at the end of a long and hard week while relaxing into the ethereal, mathematical beauty of Bach's 'Goldberg Variations'. Standing at the tomb of Archbishop Oscar Romero, courageous spokesman of the poor during El Salvador's terrible civil war of the 1970s, gunned down by assassins even as he raised the host at Mass in a hospice chapel in San Salvador.

And other moments too, in places hallowed by people's sense of the presence of God – in a Cotswold church on a Sunday morning in the very English ordinariness of a place used for worship for a thousand years – in the Basilica of St Francis at Assisi, in front of a Cimabue fresco of the Madonna and angels that has a beauty which still shimmers after seven hundred years – in the quiet of the modern Memorial Church in Berlin, bathed in subdued light cast by deep-blue stained glass, in the heart of a busy modern city and surrounded by reminders of tragedy and evil – or at the Easter Saturday vigil at the Wangfoujing Catholic Church of Beijing, jam-packed with Chinese of all ages gathered in the candle-lit darkness for the drama of resurrection.

And many other moments over the years. Different sorts of moments. T. S. Eliot's 'moments in and out of time'. Such moments are ones to which I might want to say, 'But stay awhile . . .' – but if I do, it is not Mephistopheles I am dealing with.

This does have content, though. This is belief, not just experience or feeling. And my belief is, by choice and not by inheritance or by easy certainty, Christian. It defines my end, in the end, and therefore it is my beginning on the journey. This has implications – for an understanding of human nature, experience and history, and for self-understanding. It is a metaphysical and moral framework which constitutes an interpretative prism for me. I am bound to seek to interpret history, to evaluate my experience of my working life, and to reflect on life's choices through that prism, using its imagery and wisdom.

For one thing, it militates against the reductionism that takes all sorts of guises: the view that experience and history are just serendipity; the view that sees the human mind as just a series of electrical impulses in the brain; or human consciousness as just a sequence of moments which we delude ourselves into seeing as connected experiences of a person; or a Monet painting as just an array of chemical pigments; or life as just 'one damn thing after another'. The devil is in that word 'just'.

This is metaphysics which contests the reductionism of that word 'just' – metaphysics for which the value of life is intense, and in which goodness, beauty and creativity are an intrinsic potential of the human experience of being. 'I have come that people may have life, and have it in all its fullness.' But just as the value of the human spirit, with all its possibilities for goodness and creativity, is so intensely real, seen through the Christian prism, so also is the potential of evil and destructiveness. Notoriously, Christian metaphysics makes no serious attempt to explain the origin or cause of evil: it simply asserts its reality. The serpent is just there in the Garden of Eden. The legend of Lucifer – the light-bearer, whose divine ambition is his downfall – merely attributes human failings to an angelic being, in the same way that Greek myths transposed human passions on to the gods. It does not explain. But the Christian understanding of the nature of humanity insists on the reality of the experience of evil. It does not explain it, but it will not deny its existence.

Which brings us to the first of those three ambiguities – the fact that everything we experience is shot through with imperfection. Why is it that this seems to be so much the natural order of things? Why is humanity capable of reaching such heights and plumbing such depths? Shakespeare has Hamlet muse on human nature:

What a piece of work is a man! How noble in reason, how infinite in faculties, in form and moving how express and admirable, in action how like an angel, in apprehension how like a god! – the beauty of the world, the paragon of animals! And yet to me what is this quintessence of dust?

But this is somehow only the half of it. It is not that the glory of humankind is really nothing but worthless dust. The truth is more uncomfortable than that. From great events of history to mundane moments of individual lives, we show ourselves capable of using our creative potential in limitless deceit, hatred, greed and savagery. All the signs are that this has been so from the dawn of recorded history. For the last two thousand years, history can seem to be a history of slaughter that reads like an atlas of Eurasia – there are so many cities where blood has famously run in the streets, from Europe through the Middle East, to China and beyond. Nor are such events somehow different in kind from the many deeds of shame which disfigure ordinary lives in more prosaic times: they are just at one end of the spectrum.

Human wrong-doing and cruelty manifests itself among children at play, between husband and wife, in social exclusion, in work life, in commerce. In virtually any realm of activity, we are led to say, 'At our best ... at our worst ...' At its best, the parent–child relationship has a divine touch to it; it is a real insight into the divine vulnerability of love (and perhaps into the vulnerability of even divine love). At its worst, it can have an intense and unforgivable cruelty to it. And the same goes in the more arms-length world of business life, in the markets and the commerce which touch us all. At its best, as we have seen, there is no more powerful engine for development and liberation than the market. At its worst, it is a dangerous moral pollutant which nourishes some very poisonous weeds in us.

This is all of a piece. One of the recurring themes of this book is that we are all increasingly connected through the process of globalization. But there is another sense too in which our connectedness is a fact, and has been since the dawn of human interaction: we are all caught up in the same web. 'At our best ... at our worst ...' applies in some measure to all of us. It is as if both wheat and tares grow in all our lives – in each of us individually, and down history – perhaps to the end of time. Globalization as a human phenomenon, and any venture we undertake in the context of it, is bound to reflect this ambiguity of imperfection.

And biblical imagery understands this perfectly. It begins with a clear sense of the preciousness of humanity. To take but one passage of lyrical beauty, Psalm 8 has this to say about human value:

> I look up at your heavens, shaped by your fingers,
>   at the moon and the stars you set firm –
> what are human beings that you spare a thought for them,
>   or the child of Adam that you care for him?

> Yet you have made him little less than a god,
>> you have crowned him with glory and beauty,
> made him lord of the works of your hands,
>> put all things under his feet . . .

Of course, the history of actual human beings and their behaviour comes rapidly down to earth. The story of the people in the Old Testament is the story of a people whose chosenness lies not in being different from others, but precisely in being representative because they are so exactly like others. Their leaders were often greedy, philandering, corrupt, violent – all the things that people with power and wealth so often are. Those who were led were fickle, and no doubt did many of the same things as their leaders on a smaller scale.

The only thing that was extraordinary about this commonplace history was the unique response it provoked from a group of figures known as the prophets – who were sometimes solitary outsiders, but sometimes even establishment figures. Through generations, they kept up a critique of all that was going on – often powerfully expressed in poetry which stands comparison with the greatest literature of any human culture – in the name of their God.

No other culture produced anything quite like this. An early, and angry, voice was that of Amos the farmer, incensed by the corrupt urban world of the religious and cultural elite in Jerusalem:

> Spare me the din of your chanting,
>> Let me hear none of your strumming on lyres,
> But let justice flow like water,
>> And uprightness like a never-failing stream.

As the centuries wore on, and human nature failed to change its spots, the voices of protest were raised again and again – from the plaintive, to the angry, to the outraged. In literary terms, the finest example is the Book of Isaiah – itself a compilation from roughly the same period in human history that saw the emergence of the *Iliad* in Greece. The sense of disappointment at the spiritual and moral failure of human beings who are given all they need for a good life haunts, for instance, this imagined court scene where God as plaintiff brings his case before the people (who, in a dramatic irony, are the defendants):

> My beloved had a vineyard
>   On a fertile hillside.
> He dug it, cleared it of stones,
>   And planted it with red grapes.
> In the middle he built a tower,
>   He hewed a press there too.
> He expected it to yield fine grapes:
>   [But] wild grapes were all it yielded.
>
> And now citizens of Jerusalem
>   And people of Judah,
> I ask you to judge between me
>   And my vineyard.
> What more could I have done for my vineyard
>   That I have not done?
> Why, when I expected it to yield fine grapes,
>   Has it yielded wild ones?

Here the tone is pleading. At the other end of the scale is, for example, the literary violence of the attack on the people's moral and spiritual infidelity to be found in the Book of Ezekiel. At one point, the people are portrayed by the metaphor of a young woman raised from helpless babyhood through adolescence to become a bride richly adorned by God – but whose libido then leads her into a wild sexual rampage. Even prostitutes expect to be paid, whereas she actually pays her lovers to come to her. This is not a passage for the squeamish.

Also to be found in the imagery of the Old Testament is a striking sense that the paths of glory lead but to the grave. Ecclesiastes, the Book of the Preacher, can sound like a voice out of time: the sense of the vanity of toil, given the changes and chances of life, and the inevitability of death, echoes over the millennia as strongly as ever:

Remember your creator in the days of your youth, before the days of trouble come, and the years draw near when you will say, 'I have no pleasure in them'; before the sun and the light and the moon are darkened and the clouds return with the rain; on the day when the guards of the house tremble, and the strong men are bent, and the women who grind cease working because they are few, and those who look through the windows see dimly: ... before the silver cord is snapped, and the golden bowl is broken, and the pitcher is broken at the fountain, and the wheel broken at the cistern, and the dust returns to the earth as it was, and the breath returns to God who gave it. Vanity of vanities, says the Teacher; all is vanity.

One way and another, this imagery – arising partly from that extraordinary dialectic between the prophets and the people, and partly from the sort of 'wisdom' reflected in Ecclesiastes (whose themes can be found in other cultures too, of course) – holds together two enduring truths about humanity which are in perpetual tension. Humankind – collectively and individually – is both infinitely precious and perennially wayward, forever striving after the vanities of life, for that which is transient and cannot satisfy. To use the terms of Christian theology: humankind simultaneously bears the marks of original *grace* and original *sin*.

Sin is a concept which sits uneasily with the modern, secularized, mind. In popular usage it is widely debased, used (often with more than a whiff of ridicule) of specific actions, but not in its generic sense of a proclivity to wrong-doing. To the humanist, the idea of a proclivity to wrong can seem at best pessimistic and at worst obscurantist nonsense used to cow people. To the determinist looking to explain as much of human behaviour as possible in terms of sociology, psychology and neurology, it can easily seem to be nothing more than unnecessary, pre-scientific conceptual baggage – as worthless as the Ptolemaic system of cosmology.

But its interpretive power is compelling. It is naive optimism about ourselves and our histories which has been made bankrupt by the upheavals unleashed in the process of globalization, commercialization and urbanization – not the concept of original sin, which we go on confirming in countless different ways with every year that goes by.

It is striking that, while popular usage has debased the idea of sin, evil is a concept which retains its power to bring us up short. We remain both fascinated and nonplussed by it, as we repeatedly find it not just 'out there' in some supernatural guise, nor 'just there' in some nightmarish historical event that we can ring-fence because we were not involved, but in us and among us – alongside the creativity and beauty which are the hallmarks of our original grace.

For me, this truth is powerfully in evidence in a particular place: Weimar, in Germany – home of Goethe as he wrote his *Faust*, a magnet for the literati of eighteenth- and nineteenth-century Europe, a sort of pretty German Stratford-upon-Avon.

To the north of this idyllic town lies the Etterberg, the wooded hill where Goethe used to ride with members of the ducal household. There is a clearing in the midst of this wooded upland which is nowadays just a flat, gravel-covered space with a handful of buildings in one corner – all that is left of one of the more notorious concentration camps: Buchenwald (which means, simply, 'Beech Wood'). During the course of its eight-year existence, Buchenwald housed about a quarter of a million people. Although it was not an extermination camp in the manner of Auschwitz or Treblinka, people were systematically degraded and brutalized there, and died, or were killed, in their tens of thousands.

Beyond the brutal hard labour, the experiments and the murders, though, it is the bureaucracy of the whole place that is especially mind-numbing – the regular returns neatly filled out on standard forms: opening total, plus number in (by type of prisoner), minus numbers out (transfers to other camps), minus deaths (often attributed conveniently to influenza), equals closing balance. And when the camp was first established, a lengthy correspondence developed between the camp commander and his Berlin masters as to what it should be called. Not Etterberg or Weimar: either name would associate it too closely with the cultural legacy of Goethe. Not after the nearest small village – because in that case only rural rates of pay would apply, not the higher urban rates. In the end, it was agreed that the formal name would be 'Buchenwald, postal district Weimar' – which was enough to get the urban allowances paid; and since the name would in practice be shortened to 'Buchenwald', the cultural sensitivities would be spared.

That this discussion could be carried on in such a bureaucratic tone, avoiding any reference to what the camp actually was, is almost as sinister as the activity carried out there – because it is so unsettlingly normal. We tell ourselves we cannot imagine working with human skin as if it were leather. But perhaps I *can* see myself getting caught up in such an ordinary procedure as this. I can see myself losing sight of ulterior objectives, motives, values – becoming so engrossed in a debate about whether regulation A or B applies in situation X, that I no longer notice what X actually stands for.

And in fact we forget about ends and values all the time. It is so easy to do. You don't need to be a concentration-camp official to become too absorbed in making situation X work. What is more, situation X may not be so different from normality as was Buchenwald from Weimar: the difference in ends and values may be subtler, and may also widen only gradually. Like the frog in the water that comes slowly to the boil, we may not even notice the change that kills our spirits.

How can we react adequately, then, to this forbidding place? Not by pretending we are just observers. By what evil twist do the names of Weimar and Buchenwald end up being so irrevocably linked. Why is such evil *juxtaposed* with such beauty and creativity? Why does the evil manifest itself not only in the horrendous activity; but also in bureaucratic ordinariness? Answer: none of us can distance ourselves from the human nature which makes it all possible. An honest encounter with this place is a confrontation with our species and our selves. For there is surely no more vivid (and ironic) picture of the human spirit than this tableau in two parts. Napoleon remarked, to the Polish ambassador D. G. de Pradt following the retreat from Moscow in 1812, that 'from the sublime to the ridiculous there is only one step.' But this is not the ridiculous. The sublime and the evil are close to each other too. From Weimar to Buchenwald is 5 km: a short enough distance to travel ... And we are all at risk of making that journey.

Original grace and original sin: the original ambiguity about human beings – about all of us in whatever we do. It seems to be with us always, and it underlies our personal disappointment with ourselves, our awareness of ideals we fall short of, our sense of injustice and wrong (in others and in ourselves), our sense of dissatisfaction and transience, our awareness of the reality of evil. As globalization unfolds and challenges the human condition itself, we learn more and more about what we are capable of – for good and for ill – and what we learn is in fact an old truth, an old dilemma, embedded in the whole history of the human species, and given voice in passages of creative beauty, in poetry of indignant anger and in reflective existential wisdom, in those extraordinary ancient writings from the Bible. Their resonance doesn't fade with time. For the truth about original grace and original sin is as relevant today in a twenty-first century, globally connected world as it was in the time of Isaiah or Ecclesiastes.

And what of the outcome – the endgame – of globalization? Our sense of ambiguity about human development and where it is taking us is very live of course. Indeed, it has rarely been more intense than it has of late, in the midst of a global financial and economic crisis which has seen such a wholesale collapse of trust and confidence, and against the background of rising concern about our whole impact on the planet.

And, again, nothing is new under the sun. That ambiguity about the end of it all, which we feel so acutely when the process of globalization seems, at least for a while, to have lost its way, is perfectly reflected in the ambiguity of the biblical imagery of the endgame. Is it to be some dreadful apocalypse (the word means 'lifting of the veil')? You can find graphic visions of a fiery end-time in both the Old Testament and the New. There have always been those who have sought signs in such visions, who have approached them with a crass literalism and treated them as having some sort of uncanny predictive power. But their real relevance – their real power – comes not from such nonsense, but from the way in which these visions give vivid form to our deepest fears: our fear that we are riding a tiger; that the cup is not merely half-empty rather than half-full but that it is a cup of bile we are being forced to drink; that, when weighed in the balance, human suffering exceeds human contentment, and evil is gaining the upper hand over the good. 'Apocalypse' is by no means a dead word in modern thought.

And on the other hand you can also find quite different images of the endgame. Isaiah's vision of the peaceable kingdom sounds like a classical Virgilian Arcadia. Its specific imagery is unrealistic, yet not surreal. It should be taken no more literally than the apocalyptic imagery, but the atmosphere it conjures up is just as powerful, although utterly different:

> The wolf shall live with the lamb,
> the leopard shall lie down with the kid,
> the calf and the lion and the fatling together,
> and a little child shall lead them.
> The cow and the bear shall graze,
> their young shall lie down together;
> and the lion shall eat straw like the ox.
> The nursing child shall play over the hole of the asp,
> and the weaned child shall put its hand on the adder's den.
> They will not hurt or destroy
> on all my holy mountain;
> for the earth will be full of the knowledge of the Lord
> as the waters cover the sea.

Here is a vision of a consummation in which the common good triumphs over evil, of suffering and pain eliminated, of a new paradise. It is purely forward-looking – no hint here of turning back to some golden age of the past. The vision is not of a rediscovered Garden of Eden, nor of some beautiful afterlife in some Elysian field, but of a new era of this-worldly human experience.

Even without taking the details of its vision of natural transformation too literally, we can see clearly how this gives colour to some of our deepest yearnings – for a life of harmony and balance among humans and with our natural environment; for an end in the future which gives purpose to the struggles of the present and helps us deal with its wrongs and disappointments. To a humankind which is increasingly urbanized and feels it is a threat to its own environment, this vision becomes more and more powerful as the years go by.

The point is that the ambiguity about the destination which we so deeply feel is clearly reflected in the vivid (and sometimes lurid) imagery of the Bible. Seen through that prism, the question remains open and puts in question any cavalier optimism about progress. If we have doubts, we have them on the highest authority.

Yet this is not all. Beyond the ambiguity about human nature and the ambiguity about the endgame, there is a third – and crucial – motif of the biblical story which is directly relevant to this interpretation of and response to our increasingly globalized world of experience. For again and again, amid disappointment and in the teeth of the evidence, hope shows its face.

The imagery of hope shines through in both the Old Testament and the New. And it does so in ways which are at once very specific and this-worldly and at the same time ambitious aspirations. Seemingly doomed to constant disappointment, these aspirations remain as relevant and challenging now as they were when first expressed. From the world of the prophets, for example, the following image was so striking from the first that it is ascribed to two different prophets and picked up in two different prophetic books, Micah and Isaiah:

> they shall beat their swords into ploughshares
>   and their spears into pruning-hooks;
> nation shall not lift up sword against nation,
>   neither shall they learn war any more.

The only things that have changed, two and a half millennia later, are the technology of combat and of peaceable production, and the globalized scale of the risks of conflict.

There is similarly specific imagery of hope in the New Testament. Here the thought-world has evolved – partly because it is half a millennium later, and partly because it reflects a new Christian perspective, rooted in that Old Testament background, but growing with its own dynamic. The frame of reference has become altogether more cosmopolitan. St Paul is a controversial figure in the modern world for many reasons – so much so that it is all too easy to over-look the extent to which he spoke for a world which was even then becoming more urban and more connected through trade and the movement of people. He lived at a time when the Roman Empire was at its zenith and when Greeks had spread round the Mediterranean, with their trade and their ideas. His vision of the social implications of Christianity in this rapidly evolving milieu is striking for its radicalism: 'There is no longer Jew or Greek, there is no longer slave or free, there is no longer male and female; for all of you are one in Christ Jesus.'

Thus in essence Paul wishes away the three great divides which have fractured every human civilization down the ages, one way or another, and whose continued existence is a standing reminder of how far we still have to travel on the road to a peaceful, just, global end point. These three great divides – based on race/culture, on social class, and on gender – continue to be evident almost everywhere. We may well feel that Paul's other writings are not always fully con-sistent with this vision. We will certainly recognize that the Christian movement in history has fallen woefully short of this ideal on all three counts. But the ideal, and the hope, stand the test of time.

Progress has certainly been made. Britain, for example, is far less racist, class-ridden and sexist than it was just a generation ago. And analogous changes have taken place in many countries throughout the world. Attitudes that were prevalent and would have been expressed with no sense of shame or embarrassment just a hundred years ago would make us wince now. Social commentators are often more conscious of the extent to which the situation still falls short of the ideal, but the progress is real and significant nonetheless. And it is largely the result of the forces of commercialization, urbanization and individualization, which are such powerfully transforming elements of globalization.

But we are not there yet, and we need to keep the flame of hope burning. Each of these topics – race/culture, social divisions, and gender – would warrant a book in itself. From the perspective of this chapter of this book, however, it is the overriding importance of the last one – gender – which needs special emphasis.

Throughout history from the very earliest times, in every culture until very recent times, and in many cultures to this day, one half of the population has been treated as in subjection to the other half at every level of society, and has been used and abused accordingly. The occasional exceptions – Queen Elizabeth I of England, Catherine the Great of Russia, and the Dowager Empress Cixi of China – prove the rule. There may have been households at all times and in all places where a woman ruled from behind the scenes. There have always been families in which traditional roles have been filled comfortably by men and women, brothers and sisters. There have probably always been families where shared leadership – genuine partnership – has been realized in practice, whatever the social norms. But the overwhelming fact is that for most of history the vast majority of women have played a marginal role in society, have been denied education or any serious chance to achieve their potential, and have lived in a domestic subjection which gave them few rights. Often the subjection has been enforced with specific cruelty: suttee, foot-binding, female circumcision, female infanticide, forced marriages – all of which have contributed to immeasurable suffering and waste of human potential.

It is one of the most striking glories of globalization that the processes of urbanization, education and communication are gradually righting this huge wrong. As even the poorest and most rural communities start to be connected, for example through the extension of microfinance, we find – as shown in Chapter 6 – that women become empowered. And, lo and behold, the world discovers that women can flourish and lead commercially, professionally, politically – in any of the realms of activity that men down through history have seen fit to arrogate to themselves.

But there is yet a deeper truth to be discerned in this most profound of social changes being ushered in through globalization. This truth is implicit in that vision of St Paul: for it is not a matter simply of women claiming their rights and men having to move over to make room for them on the social stage. What is implicit in Paul's language, I believe, is the potential for human social interaction to take on a new and better quality through the free and full involvement of both male and female perspectives. It is as if the human personality – whether in a man or a woman – needs for its own wholeness to discover in itself the different emphases we have traditionally associated with male and female types.

Just as ideas about femininity have often been used to dehumanize women by depicting them as irrational, emotional, weak and help-less, so stereotypical ideas about masculinity have dehumanized men by depicting them as independent, assertive, strong and heroic – and therefore bound to fail. Modern science has shown psychological happiness to depend on a much greater awareness of so-called 'male' and 'female' qualities running through all humanity. If men were to be unchanged by the full participation of women in public life, if women were to participate in public life on the basis of adoption of traditional male modes of interaction, then humankind would have missed a profoundly important opportunity for growth. All the evidence is that something far better is achievable: any business leader, for example, will attest that the dynamic of working groups (at any level of enterprise, from boards of governance to the smallest ad-hoc project group) is improved by the presence of both men and women.

There is no question that this is one of the most significant senses in which Teilhard de Chardin's insight is true – that the human becomes a person not just as individual, but in community. Teilhard saw community as emerging through the growing global connected-ness of humankind (not as a reversion to earlier, small-scale, separated communitarian living). This community is by definition borderless, and cannot be exclusive. And by definition it has to have the full participation of personalities made individual (and therefore open) by the same process of globalization. 'No man is an island.' And no woman either. We will have reached the Omega Point when St Paul's vision is finally realized.

This is also the hope which lies implicit, I believe, in those mysterious lines which bring Goethe's monumental *Faust* to its conclusion. If ever there was a figure who embodies a titanic male assertiveness, it is Goethe's protagonist. There is no sign that he has any instinct for a more holistic view of human self-actualization and fulfilment. Helen of Troy is an ideal, not a real person. Gretchen is all too real, and is crushed by him. Yet she finds redemption, and in his final, ambiguous assumption at the point of death Faust hears her welcome, and the 'mystical chorus' closes this whole extra-ordinary saga with lines which can be seen as pointing to that same vision which is explicit in St Paul and implicit in Teilhard de Chardin. 'The eternal feminine draws us on'.

Is this hope just naive? Is there no longer Jew or Greek, no longer slave or free? No longer male or female? We are hardly there yet. And, in the stress of daily battle, progress is often indiscernible. What, therefore, is the basis of this irrational hope?

Through a Christian prism, I have to interpret the history and find the basis for that hope in one central image above all. It takes me back to that visit to Milan Cathedral and to that crucifix hanging silently in the interior gloom of the nave. We are too familiar with the symbol, really. As an image, the cross is both common through-out much of the world and in competition for people's attention with other images that are also increasingly global – religious, secular and commercial. For many its significance is barely understood and elicits less recognition than the Golden Arches (which are now more ubiquitous). For some its significance is vitiated by history (its association with the crusades in the Middle East, for example). For others it serves as a talisman and/or badge of identity over and against others – witness, for example, the sight in the 1990s of the Serbians fighting in Bosnia wearing crucifixes prominently around their necks.

But the cross was in fact an instrument of execution – and a commonplace one at that. We have forgotten how shocking it must have been to take this instrument as a sign for a new movement, as a sign of hope. As this movement's leader and inspiration is put to death on this device, he cries out two things that show us just how extraordinary this sign of hope is. 'My God, my God, why have you forsaken me?' This bleak cry takes us to the very limit of the experience of failure, despair and loneliness. Many of us have had or will have had the experience: and even those of us who don't know that many do. And we are necessarily involved as humans – no story of our globalization is complete without it.

Then there is that final cry: according to St John's Gospel, 'It is finished!' – actually, 'It is accomplished' – even in the moment of death. What on earth could it mean – at that particular moment? This is not the place for a theological discussion of that question. Millions of words have been written down the centuries of Christian history on the significance of that death. Different perspectives, different theories have sought to articulate and explain it. I doubt if they could ever plumb its depths fully. And, in any case, however we seek to describe it theologically is of no account if it does not strike us at the centre of our being. And I cannot see how it can do that without becoming *the* prism of hope through which we see ourselves and our world – hope that persists in the midst of *anything* that human experience offers up, on the grounds of what was accomplished there, at that point in time. Hence the relevance of the crucifix in Milan Cathedral and in every other setting where we find it. Again, we are necessarily involved, as human beings. And no story of our globalization can be completed without it.

And so, in the final analysis, we confront our globalizing future, individual and collective, material and spiritual, with hope – not with despair, and not with uncritical optimism.

This is in turn a challenge to action – in all realms of life, including the realm of the intimate, of society, of commerce, of work, and also in our inner selves (which are not known fully even to ourselves). The challenge confronts us in several senses. First, we are called to engagement, not disengagement – into life in the ambiguous bazaar, not out of it. It is also a challenge of judgement: it is salutary at a time of global crisis to remember that the very word 'crisis' comes from the Greek for 'judgement'. As long as we are involved, directly or indirectly, in injustice, exclusion and exploitation – which will be always – it is inevitable that judgement be part of our experience. Then, thirdly, each of us may have to carry our own personal cross, and we may not be able to predict how, why or when. In that experience, we may have to hold on to the recognition that this has been done before. And, finally, we know for sure that we will stumble; but that remorse is always an option, atonement and renewal are always possible. Even when something feels like the end, it can be the beginning.

On this basis, we will not cease from exploration (and striving), though we will not see the end. And even though we only have an incomplete and provisional understanding of the direction and destination, we have it in our power to hope for progress towards it – which is the only responsible vision for life in the global bazaar.

Acknowledgements

Acknowledgement is due to the copyright holders of the following works for their kind permission to reprint extracts in this book:

T. S. Eliot, 'Little Gidding', 'Journey of the Magi', *Four Quartets*, and 'Choruses from *The Rock*', in *The Complete Poems and Plays of T. S. Eliot* (London: Faber and Faber, 2004). Extracts reproduced by permission of Faber and Faber Ltd.

Samuel Beckett, *Waiting for Godot* (London: Faber and Faber, 2006). Extract reproduced by permission of Faber and Faber Ltd.

Peter Porter, 'Your Attention Please', in *A Selected Porter* (Oxford: Oxford University Press, 1989). Extract reproduced by permission of Oxford University Press.

Teilhard de Chardin, *The Phenomenon of Man* (London: Harper Perennial, 2008). Extract reproduced by permission of Harper Perennial.

Amartya Sen, *Identity and Violence: The Illusion of Destiny* (New York: W. W. Norton & Co., 2006). Extract reproduced by permission of W. W. Norton & Co.

Niall Ferguson, *The Ascent of Money: A Financial History of the World* (London: Allen Lane, 2008). Extract reproduced by permission of Allen Lane.

Edward Luce and Chrystia Freeland, 'Summers backs state action', in the *Financial Times*, 8 March 2009. Extract reproduced by permission of the *Financial Times* and Lawrence Summers.

Paul Kennedy, 'Read the Big Four to Know Capital's Fate', in the *Financial Times*, 12 March 2009. Extract reproduced by permission of Paul Kennedy.

Nigel Lawson, 'Capitalism Needs a Revived Glass-Seagall', in the *Financial*

Times, 15 March 2009. Extract reproduced by permission of Nigel Lawson.

Eileen Claussen, 'Climate Change: Myths and Realities', speech presented at the Pew Center on Global Climate Change, New York, 17 July 2002. Extract reproduced by permission of the Pew Center on Global Climate Change.

Milton Friedman, 'A Friedman Doctrine: The Social Responsibility of Business is to Increase its Profits', in *New York Times Magazine*, 13 September 1970. Extract reproduced by permission of the *New York Times*.

Fareed Zakaria, 'India Rising', in *Newsweek*, 6 March 2006. Extract reproduced by permission of Newsweek, Inc.

Kaleem Books: www.kaleembooks.com. Extract reproduced by permission of Kaleem Books.

John R. Williams, *Goethe's Faust* (London: Allen & Unwin, 1987). Extracts reproduced by permission of Allen & Unwin.

Quotations from the New Revised Standard Version (Anglicized Edition) of the Bible, on pages 194, 198, 199, 200, 201, 203 and 204 are © 1989, 1995 by the National Council of the Churches of Christ in the United States of America. Used by permission. All rights reserved.

Quotations from the Jerusalem Bible on pages 191, 192 and 193 are © 1966 by Darton Longman & Todd Ltd and Doubleday & Co. Inc. Used by permission.